The
Kitchen Witch
HANDBOOK

The
Kitchen Witch
HANDBOOK

Wisdom, Recipes, and Potions for Everyday Magic at Home

Aurora Kane

wellfleet
press

CONTENTS

PROLOGUE

Why, who can take a simple dish and season it to grant your wish?
Or with a sprinkle and a stir, quiet fears to gentle purrs?
For strength or love or money spells, the cupboard's full, its magic swells.

The kitchen witch has many charms, but chief among them: Do no harm.
She welcomes all with open arms, and revels in this place of charms.
With fire, air, and water, too, what's born of Earth transforms to food—
to feed the belly, soul, and mind, to bless your heart, cast spells sublime.

With hearth and home as her domain, each kitchen witch can stake her claim
as mistress of this mystic realm, she honors Earth and heeds the Moon.
And with the seasons, as they turn, are lessons ripe we're meant to learn.
For manifesting magic well, intentions must be true and kind, and space allowed
        for you to shine.

Intentions are the seeds we plant, to feed our life, its wishes grant,
to ripen into sweet success, fulfill our dreams, see all are blessed.

Let hunger never enter here, nor thirst, nor want, nor harm, nor fear.
Let laughter, love, and plenty reign, each meal sufficient to sustain.
Bless open hearts and open minds, for deep within the magic shines,
with your first taste, your life can change, so be prepared and unafraid.

Each kitchen witch plants seeds unique, and tends them 'til they reach their peak.
The harvest is Earth's gift to use for magic cast with gratitude.

INTRODUCTION

To be a kitchen witch is to see magic and possibility in all Nature offers. To be a kitchen witch is to nourish, care for, soothe, and celebrate those who sit at your table and to share with those who cannot. To be a kitchen witch is to create magic out of the ordinary and see the ordinary as magic. To be a kitchen witch is to believe in the power of transformation and intention. To be a kitchen witch is to choose healing over harm and love over hate.

To be a kitchen witch is to live your best magical life with your kitchen as altar. It requires belief in your powers, an openness to your intuition and the messages it receives, and trust in the Universe, which can bring a sense of peace, calm, and accomplishment. To be a kitchen witch is to engage all your senses to extract meaning and purpose from everyday rituals—the most powerful of which is cooking for and sharing a meal with someone.

The kitchen is your sacred place. Nature, the elements, foods, herbs and spices, utensils, and recipes are your magical tools. Utilizing them in mindful ways means taking time to be present in each moment, to set goals and intentions based on your beliefs, hopes, and desires, and to infuse your foods and your life with the energies to manifest dreams.

Take a seat at this table and join the conversation. Learn what it means to create magic in your kitchen as you tend the cauldron of knowledge and transformation. Take your cues from the Wheel of the Year: honor the seasons and their gifts, live in rhythm with Nature, matching her ebb and flow to create space for your magic as you connect to Earth and honor the Moon's wisdom. Mother Nature will not be hurried, so delight in the pace she sets and trust that the seeds you plant will come to fruition.

Celebrate bounty. Listen for the messages these magical foods carry from Earth to your table. Feed and nourish your friends and family with meals seasoned with love, hope, luck, beauty, protection, remembrance, and any other intentions that speak your truth. Twenty-six recipes celebrate the season; add yours along the way. Use the spells, seasonal blessings, and rituals to amplify the magic of your messages or create your own. Your heart is filled with the magic you need. Don't hesitate to use it.

And remember, plants are living, breathing beings that deserve our care and respect, for they have much to teach us. They can also be harmful. Never ingest any food, herb, flower, seed, fruit, vegetable, or plant without proper knowledge of what you have and never do anything that feels intuitively wrong.

This is your domain. May it be blessed with love, joy, and plenty. May the fire burn bright and your cauldron be bottomless. May your magic be without limit.

PART 1

KITCHEN WITCHERY

The kitchen witch is a powerful being descended from centuries of wisdom, lore, and knowledge gleaned from Nature and passed on by example. Part hearth goddess, part herbal wisewoman, part mother goddess, and part intuitive being, she lives in harmony with Nature while tending hearth, cauldron, family, and garden. Her knowledge is vast and her responsibilities are many, but her purpose is singular: transformation.

This is her domain: honoring the transformation of the seasons and understanding their influence on life; clearing the cobwebs in spring and fall, planting the seeds of intentions and transforming Earth to bear fruit; tending and reaping summer's harvest, combining foods with the elements of air, water, fire, and earth as well as energetic herbs and spices to nourish a family's body and spirit to live with intention while celebrating achievements made; preserving the last of fall's harvest for overwintering, while preparing to rest and renew with gratitude for the bounty; taking stock of the year to reinforce lessons learned and plan anew as winter transforms again into spring. And along the way, honoring the natural energies of the seasons and transmuting their gifts to manifest magic, to nurture and heal, to ground and connect.

The transformative power of kitchen witchery lives in all our hearts. We just need to be still long enough to hear its call and brave enough to act. All are welcome in this witch's kitchen.

And although more modern kitchen witches may trade foraging at farmers' markets and grocery stores for planting and tending the kitchen garden, the purpose is no different and the magic no less magical. Each act is done with intention for good and abundant love, with love being the most transformative ingredient of all.

KITCHEN MAGIC

That spark. It starts it all. That spark of an idea that lights the imagination; that spark of love that never dies; that spark of a match that lights a candle dispelling darkness; that spark that lights the warming hearth fires or celebrates traditions over a campfire, or that burns steadily beneath a simmering cauldron. That spark is transformative, and so is your kitchen magic. Here, you have the ability not only to transform Nature's bounty into joy and nourishment but also to infuse that bounty with metamorphic intentions to manifest magic everywhere. That spark is magic.

For the kitchen witch, your kitchen is your altar—that place that focuses your magic and reminds you what you're working toward. It is also a place to honor memories and traditions, as well as celebrate and create new ones uniquely yours.

Practicing kitchen magic is a way to blend magic into your everyday life with little effort and great reward. It personifies the law of similarity, that like begets like. It honors the process of preparing and consuming food as well as the innate magic in every ingredient Nature gives us. It is a way to direct Nature's energy to influence magical work on your behalf, to live your best magical life, and to be your best magical self for those around you.

What is Kitchen Magic?

Whether or not you're a kitchen witch, magic happens in the Earth anywhere food is grown and in the kitchen anytime food is prepared and shared. The foods and the elements—earth, air, fire, water—combine to transform ingredients into delightful flavors and nutrients to feed and nourish our bodies and spirits. When you add intention in selecting, preserving, preparing, cooking, and sharing, plus the intentions of your heart and the foods' innate energies, you have a most magical recipe for effecting the changes you desire. Season with love, serve with care, acknowledge the time required, celebrate the bounty, and share with gratitude. That's kitchen magic.

For many who practice kitchen magic, the Wheel of the Year provides the context of living in tune with Nature's seasons, feeling the ebb and flow of the changing rhythms. It engages all our senses and affirms our connections to Earth and others. It is a way to care for our planet as it cares for us.

Food as Magic

Food *is* magic. Throughout history it has even been worshipped and revered for all sorts of things, including bringing people back from the dead and being given as offerings to appease or curry favor with myriad gods and goddesses.

It sprouts miraculously from seeds buried in the ground—whether intentionally planted or blown there by the wind and nurtured by the Sun, rain, and occasional garden fairy. It comes to us, plucked straight from Earth, full of vitamins, minerals, fiber, water, protein, sugar, fat, and other things our bodies need to grow and stay healthy. It delights every one of our senses. It is rife with ritual, defining special occasions and celebrations. It is energy that can ground, nourish, heal, delight, transport, entertain, soothe, and excite. Food creates relationships over which it is shared, memories, traditions, gifts, medicine. Science has yet to unlock all the magical secrets that foods contain and our intuition has likely just scratched the surface of their wisdom.

Food as magic adds another layer of meaning to cooking and eating. The law of vibration tells us everything vibrates as energy—energies interconnected and influenced by each other. Using food's energy with simple rituals or intentions can help send positive energy and vibrations into the Universe, where they're manifested as our dreams and desires. Food as magic can bring love, success, wealth, patience, health, empathy, courage, compassion, intuition, joy, friendship, sex, fertility and abundance, and more. Its energy is of life.

Because every food has magical properties, deciding which to include is a purely personal choice! Prepare the food with respect and honor, imbuing it with your wishes and intentions. Be mindful of the outcomes you desire and stir joy and gratitude into every spoonful.

KITCHEN MAGIC TOOLS

The most fundamental of all magical tools, the elements of earth, water, air, and fire are the basis of all kitchen magic. Earth keeps us grounded; water keeps our energy flowing and our spirits adaptable; air keeps us alive; and fire transforms, warms, and ignites our passions. Use them with gratitude and give thanks for their easy access in your life.

Other than these, no special tools are required to unleash your kitchen witchery. Use whatever you have or whatever speaks to you, but the guide on the next pages gives some ideas on kitchen rituals and equipment that can be put to use in enchanting ways.

Apron. A kitchen witch's ritual garment.

Besom (see page 73). Symbolically sweep away bad energy and cleanse your magical space. Use your trusty regular broom to sweep away the actual dirt, and make it a goal to keep this space clean and tidy so your magic flows freely.

Cauldron. As the vehicle for providing nourishment, it is a symbol of abundance, as well as knowledge and wisdom, transformation and rebirth, the home and hearth. Gather a couple of sizes—a small cauldron to keep on your altar, as well as a Dutch oven (or two) and a cast-iron skillet to conjure your magical elixirs and potions, combining food and love to feed your family.

Chalice. A favorite wineglass or teacup (see page 39) will do to sip potions, offer blessings, and divine the future. You may want to designate specific items used solely for these purposes to keep their energy clear.

Cookbooks and a journal. Whether holding your favorite recipes or the secret potions of your ancestors, keep your recipes alive by jotting notes in them of favorite times they were served, or revisions needed to make their magic more potent. Store within easy reach to keep their inspiration fresh in your mind.

Fork. Symbolic of the food you prepare intentionally to nourish body and soul.

Knife. A good chef's knife is an invaluable tool in the kitchen witch's arsenal. In the same way it chops, cuts, trims, and prepares foods, savor the symbolic imagery of it cutting away any unwanted ties that bind or negativity from your life. It can also scare away an evil spirit or two.

Mortar and pestle. Symbolizing the magic of alchemy and the wisdom of working with ingredients to heal, the mortar and pestle was also Baba Yaga's favorite mode of transportation (see page 31), perhaps, again, reminding us of the transformative power of this simple tool.

Spoon. A magic wand, indeed. A spoon can symbolize want; it also symbolizes air. Keep one nearby to remind you of the bounty you reap and the gratitude you feel for the blessings in your life. It's also useful to stir up a bit of magical energy in anything you make: clockwise to draw things to you, counterclockwise to protect from unwanted energies.

Teakettle. For making the favorite cuppa and adding a little grounding and divining ritual into any day (see page 39).

The elements. *Air*: The element of air works magic in your kitchen, and kitchen garden, to help you prepare and preserve food, whether from your oven, fridge, or freezer, or the breezes of spring, summer, and fall that tenderly encourage your growing plants. *Earth*: Whether you grow the food in your kitchen garden or pluck it fresh from the grocery store or farmers' market, the grounding, nurturing element of earth gives birth to it. *Fire*: This element ignites the magic and serves as the element of transformation. When the hearth is lit, it signals your intentions to the Universe. Let its warmth serve as a draw to gather people to this welcoming space. *Water*: To cleanse, cook, hydrate, soothe, and give life, be grateful for easy access to clean water.

Making Food More Magical

The combination of raw materials, the elements, and time creates magically transformative results, and cooking for others is one of the truest expressions of love. Food has its own kind of magic—nourishing our bodies with Nature's bounty is both healing and life giving.

Although you may wish to incorporate specific foods into your meals for their particular energies, you can also add a little magic to any food by imbuing it with your intentions and thanks before dropping it into the pot! Consider the myriad ways to bring magic to the foods you cook, serve, and share.

- Cover the table at which you eat with a tablecloth to establish the table as a "sacred space" and mark the ritual of sharing food.

- Grow your own foods in your kitchen garden (see page 53).

- Buy local and with intention.

- Cook and drink with a grateful heart. Give a short nod of gratitude to the water you drink or wash or cook food in.

- Follow the recipe (if you need to) but cook intuitively.

- Prepare foods with purpose and visualization:

  * Imaging peeling away outer layers to reveal your innermost thoughts and dreams.

  * Chop sturdy vegetables with gusto to relieve a little stress and banish negativity.

  * Wash vegetables and tender herbs gently to fill them with love.

  * Discard peels and scraps (if you can't recycle) with the intentions to discard bad habits holding you back.

  * Cut foods into magical shapes.

* Season liberally to spread the magic.

* Draw sigils on foods with condiments or a knife.

* Make extra to share.

* Stir with intention.

* Save the seeds as offerings to Nature, or to place on your altar to draw growth and prosperity.

❀ Meditate while stirring the pot, peeling vegetables, or kneading dough.

❀ Give food as gifts.

❀ Say a blessing or dedication before, or after, eating, as you like.

❀ Eat mindfully to appreciate the food and honor its gifts as well as the ritual of sharing it with others.

❀ Light candles on the table, coordinating colors with intention (see pages 20–21).

❀ Let the magic manifest according to the Universe's plan.

EATING THE RAINBOW

Eating the rainbow is a magical way not only to support your health but also to influence your kitchen magic. And color is energy. Following is a list of colors and what their innate vibrational energies support. Because colors can be assigned different or multiple meanings, and we all have memories and associations with color throughout life, experiment, have fun, and stay in tune with your intuition. Use the colors as they speak to you—and remember, at the end of each rainbow is a pot of gold.

Black: detoxifying, grounding, powerful healing, protection, security, support in grief

Blue: calm, healing, health, kindness, meditation, patience, sincerity, tranquility

Bright orange: happiness

Bright pink: creativity, glamour

Bronze/brown: clarity of thought, common sense, detoxifying, experience, grounding, longevity, prosperity, stability, strength

Dark blue: peace, spirituality, tranquility

Gold: attraction, balance, creativity, changing luck, elegance, energy, fertility, joy, prestige, prosperity, success

Green: abundance, children, Earth, feeling grounded, fertility, friendship, good luck, growth, healing, money, Nature, renewal, success, wealth

Lavender: intuition, peace, protection, spiritual growth

Orange: ambition, attraction, building energy, changing luck, courage, creativity, emotional healing, health, individuality, joy, personal power, warmth

Pink: calm, clairvoyance, compassion, faith, forgiveness, friendship, harmony, joy, tenderness

Purple: authority, intuition, prosperity, spiritual awareness, stress reduction, success, wealth, wisdom

Red/deep red: courage, motivation, passion, power, protection, romantic love, security, vitality

Silver/gray: clairvoyance, cleansing, healing, moonlight, peace, rest, sophistication, truth

Turquoise: awakening, awareness, enlightenment

Violet: creativity, dreams, healing intuition, psychic powers

White: clairvoyance, cleansing, peace, protection, security, truth; white can also stand in for any color you want but don't have. Simply visualize the desired color as you light a white candle and take a moment to imagine the outcome you wish.

Yellow: balance, communication, confidence, creativity, happiness, intuition, joy, mental clarity, optimism, personal power and self-esteem, realizing and manifesting thoughts, success in business, warmth

Reduce, Reuse, Recycle

Because the kitchen witch honors Earth and all her gifts, tending to Earth's needs is an important mission. Make it a part of your magic and of your daily kitchen rituals: Reduce waste anywhere you can, especially of life-giving foods and clean water. Reuse anything you can. Repurpose glass jars to use as storage containers or spell jars, transform leftovers, and save scraps for soups and stocks or kitchen garden compost. Eliminate single-use plastics. Recycle what you can't reuse so its useful life continues.

Cooking with Intentions

The law of vibration is the foundation of the law of attraction and tells us every "thing," like color and food, vibrates, though each thing, made differently, vibrates at different frequencies. So, too, do your intentions. This universal energy means all things are interconnected and influenced by each other, and like ripples in a pond, they expand outward. Formulating your energy-filled intentions and releasing them into the Universe allows the energy to influence the results you desire and come back to you in abundance.

As a kitchen witch, manifesting with Nature's magic to live your best magical life depends on setting intentions with the natural rhythms surrounding you: to know deep in your heart what you want or need, or what needs attention in your life, understand why you want or need it, and commit to making it happen. Reaching deep into your soul to acknowledge, without fear or judgment, what is important to you and what will make you truly happy is the next step. Defining intentions keeps us focused and living in the present, staying true to our values and dreams, and can help improve our overall sense of well-being. Draw the magic to you or send a blessing into the world—but do no harm. May you receive many blessings in return.

INTUITION

Intuition is our innate ability to tune in to the vibrations around us and sense their connections in our world. Many refer to intuition as "their gut," and learning to hear and trust your gut are important skills. You'll not only gain insights into the world around you, but you will also sense when your magic is working, or perhaps needs a boost. In addition, if your gut is warning you something is not right, take heed. It's usually right. Your intuition is the best tool in your magical bag.

CHECK YOUR ENERGY

All things vibrate with energy, but not all energy is the same. It is when energies are high, filled with intent, and then released into the Universe that the magic really starts. When energy is low, you feel off-kilter, maybe from illness, anger, jealousy, or grief, things that can block the free flow of energy and keep it in a negative state. If you feel your magic is "less than," you may want to assess your energy level. If needed, try these ideas to boost it into the positive realm of peace, gratitude, grounding, and joy.

- **Cleanse away negativity or the blues.** Open the windows and sweep your kitchen space with fresh sage branches or a besom broom, focusing on corners and closets where stagnant energy lurks. Clean the floor and the counters and clean out the refrigerator. Visualize the bad vibes being chased away, or do an emotional sweep—pause and feel gratitude for all that is good. Breathe in the fresh energy while visualizing yourself releasing any anger, hurt, fear, or negativity.

- **Set an intention for joy.** Sometimes simply recognizing the low energy state and committing to change it are all that's needed. Then, act joyful.

- **Decide what makes you happy.** Be honest, nonjudgmental, accepting, and realistic. You cannot raise your vibrational energy if your actions are in misalignment with your heart.

- **Be kind to yourself.** Accept who you are. Meditate, or explore other self-care rituals that make you feel your best. Forgive yourself and others.

- **Engage with Nature.** Take a walk in Nature, or tend to your kitchen garden, and spend time listening to her musings!

The
KITCHEN WITCH
& HER DOMAIN

Historically, a home's hearth, or fireplace, was not only the place to light the fire to keep the home warm, but also the place to prepare and cook the family's food. It was typically the warmest place in the house and so the place where people gathered. It was the center of activity and the center of the home, the heart, which beat with the rhythm of the family.

Today's kitchen, though fortunately no longer the sole source of a home's heat, is no less busy. It is still a place where family and friends gather to share food, create memories, tell stories, and live life. There is an irresistible pull to this place, as if our heart recognizes another. Your kitchen is the heart of your home and the place from which your family's energy flows. It's the place where not only are our bodies nourished, but also our relationships, our spirits, our souls, our histories, our dreams, and our imaginations.

As the domain of the kitchen witch, the kitchen also represents *your* heart—tend them both wisely.

A Kitchen Altar

Though for the kitchen witch the entire kitchen is her altar, that place where the magic happens, it's also good and common practice to set up a separate space to serve as your personal altar—and, in fact, it may not be your only altar. That space can become a visual and transformative reminder of intentions set and priorities lived every day, a place to focus your energy and express your gratitude, and a place to celebrate your status as a kitchen goddess.

The space devoted to this altar does not have to be much, but it should be placed where you'll see it and where it is less likely to be disturbed by others who may also use the space. It can be as simple as a small plate or bowl holding designated items, such as a statue of your favorite kitchen goddess, or left empty to receive the changing energies each day brings. Be as fancy, creative, or minimalist as you like.

Physically cleaning the space where your altar resides and keeping it tidy removes negative energy and makes space for the good vibes to live. Keep the elements that make up your altar as natural as possible for their innate and individual energies, but always use what speaks to you. Other things to consider adding to your kitchen altar include:

- Salt, for its healing and protective abilities.

- Something fresh and green, such as a pot of herbs growing (if you have the sunlight needed) representing the element earth and its ability to ground you.

- A candle, representing the fire element and which you can light to signal releasing your intentions into the world.

- Water, for its life-giving properties and ability to enhance your intuition; make it Moon water (water infused overnight with the Full Moon's power) for extra enchantment.

- Something representative of air, such as a wand, spoon, or bell.

- A small cauldron.

- A besom.

- Small offerings, such as found things like nuts, stones, feathers, and pine cones, to the spirits who led you to them.

- A bowl of fresh fruit.

- A favorite cookbook (or two or three!).

- A mortar and pestle.

- Favorite, much-used spices.

- Photos of loved ones for whom you work your kitchen magic.

- A favorite crystal, or any you like to see or work with to raise the loving vibrations.

- Anything that makes you smile.

- A kitchen witch doll for good luck.

And, of course, change what you display on your altar based on the seasons, the Wheel of the Year, or other celebrations that are important to you. Remember, your altar represents you—your heart, hopes, dreams, intentions, and life. If you stay true to those things, it should be ready to help you work your kitchen magic any time.

The Goddess Connection: Kitchen Goddesses

Aside from your kitchen goddess self, there is a pantheon of ancient goddesses whose responsibilities and powers centered on the kitchen. From the kitchen's hearth and its fire to the cauldron of food and knowledge tended there to individual foods, their harvest, and agriculture as a whole, these deities understood the importance of this realm to the sustenance of family and community and the need to tend its spirit daily. And although the work of the kitchen goddess can feel lonely and unending, these wise and generous figures are always available to lend support and help boost your intuition, intentions, and magic when its sparkle dims. Let's explore a sample to fire up your imagination.

Airmid (Celtic) One of the mythological Tuatha Dé Danann, this Celtic goddess of herbs was renowned for her healing powers. Summon Airmid's healing wisdom when using any herbs in your kitchen.

Aphrodite (Greek)/Venus (Roman) This goddess of love, renowned for her beauty, also had responsibility for all vegetation on Earth. When matters of love are top of mind, turn to her wisdom.

Aranyani (Hindu) This goddess of the forest and all its animal inhabitants also provided food for humanity. Connecting with her fearless energies can be as simple as a walk among Nature.

Baba Yaga (Slavic/Russian) This independent figure, whose name may mean "Grandmother Witch," dwells in the forest in a hut supported by chicken legs, guarding the entrance from this world to the next. She spends her days crafting busily at the stove or sailing the skies on her mortar and pestle, using a broom to sweep away any evidence of flight. Call on Baba Yaga when the wisdom that comes with age, and typically without judgment, can offer another perspective.

Bao Gu (Chinese) Her extraordinary kindness and healing skills were legendary, especially her use of traditional Chinese medicine techniques, including the natural healing powers of herbs and water. Call on Bao Gu to summon the kindness that can sometimes cure anything.

Bastet/Bast (Egyptian) Bastet was a passionate protector of cats, women's secrets, home, and family. Call on Bastet to add a little catnip to your potions, or when the claws need to come out in the form of defense and protection.

Berchta (Germanic) This Triple Goddess of abundance and tender of gardens is celebrated from winter solstice through the New Year with a mother's dinner. All work ceases in the home and fish soup is served in her honor. Ditch the housework, order takeout, and make a toast to Berchta.

Cerridwen (Celtic) This multifaceted goddess was one of the most powerful witches in Celtic mythology, embodying all three aspects of the Triple Goddess. Among the realms she ruled were the Moon and Nature. She also watchfully tended her great cauldron of wisdom, symbolic of transformation and rebirth, in which her herbal potions transformed into potent potables that delivered beauty, imparted wisdom, and nourished inspiration. In whatever way you need, Cerridwen's magic can nourish when you feel depleted.

Circe (Greek) This goddess of magic and patron of ancient Greek witches held an enormous amount of knowledge of herbs and ways to use them in rituals, magic, and healing. When your life, or your magic, needs a little boost, invite Circe in.

Corn Mother (Native American) Like all goddesses, Corn Mother has influence over many areas: fertility, children, abundance, healing, fate, and more. She is credited by Indigenous North American agricultural tribes as being both the first woman and for giving birth to corn, with its life-sustaining nourishment and symbolism of sacred knowledge. Call on Corn Mother to nourish you in any way that sustains. Lammas celebrates the early harvest and Corn Mother.

Demeter (Greek)/Ceres (Roman) Goddess of fertility in agriculture and the harvest, Demeter rules the seasons—from birth to death and rebirth—among other things. Ceres, appropriately, lends her name to cereal, from the grains of the harvest.

Demeter's daughter, Persephone, was abducted by Hades to his Underworld to be his wife, which caused Demeter much suffering. In her grief, she forsook her goddess duties—the crops suffered, the people suffered, but Demeter continued to mourn. Hades finally agreed to release Persephone—but not without a compromise: She could return to Earth for part of the year (spring, summer, and autumn), spending the remaining time (winter) with Hades in the Underworld. Demeter is worshipped on Persephone's return in the spring and again on her departure in autumn.

Call on Demeter for her ability to relieve suffering, her wisdom in tending the harvest, her undying mother's love, and when the transition of the seasons might bring on a change of mood that needs adjusting.

Frigg/Freya (Norse) Frigg—wife of Odin, the most powerful Norse god—is the chief domestic officer, holding sway over love, home, and family. As nurturing ruler of the hearth, she is the model of domesticity and hospitality. Seek her wisdom in matters of hearth and home and invite her in any time your goddess energies are running low. Winter solstice marks the time to honor Frigg.

Gabija (Lithuanian) Goddess of the home fires and guardian of home and family, Gabija has a fiery spirit and must be tended to accordingly. When put to bed at the end of each day, her ashes are neatly swept to smolder through the night, she is given a bowl of fresh water with which to bathe, and is kindly asked to stay put. Call on Gabija for protection of the home and family, especially from thieves and evil forces. Seek her light at new beginnings or when darkness temporarily obscures your intuition.

Gaia (Greek/Roman) Representing Mother Earth, Gaia is the goddess of prophecy and the personification of abundance, represented by the cornucopia. Her specialty was growing plants used in potions to inspire enchantment. Call her into your world when things seem less than enchanted.

Hestia (Greek)/Vesta (Roman) The original domestic goddess, Hestia was a virgin goddess dedicated to the hearth, home, family, and community who was widely worshipped and held sacred in the home. Offerings of wine and food were typical, with toasts beginning and ending with "to Hestia!" Call on Hestia to help keep the fires burning within to motivate and spur you to action toward your goals.

Lakshmi (Hindu) The beautiful Hindu goddess Lakshmi, partner to Vishnu, is goddess of abundance and is honored during the yearly Diwali festival, the festival of lights. Call on Lakshmi for help manifesting intentions born of a true heart and sought with true desire.

Mawu (West African) Mother Earth goddess Mawu is creator of all life; she inspires passion, creative energy, birth, abundance, and the pregnant possibilities of hope. Mawu offers the lessons of living in harmony with Nature as well as savoring the expectant joys that life brings. Call on Mawu when you need help delivering new ideas into existence or when your burden feels too heavy to bear alone.

Pachamama (Andean) Pachamama is Earth Mother and goddess of abundance, whose greatest power is to create, preserve, and sustain life. She embodies the whole of the divine feminine and is at watch over issues of fertility, crops, and abundance. As the provider of all we need to live, call on Pachamama for any intentions, but especially when nourishment is required, whether it be spiritual, psychological, familial, or bodily. August 1, Lammas (a.k.a. Lughnasadh), honors the abundance of Pachamama.

Persephone/Proserpina (Greek) Persephone, wife of Hades, was the goddess of vegetation, particularly grain. Her symbolism is that of the return of spring, as she was allowed back to Earth, from the Underworld, once a year, when the world burst again into bloom. When the need for rejuvenation or rebirth is of import, call on Persephone.

Pomona (Roman) Although Pomona was a protective spirit of the home, her main responsibility was tending the orchards and gardens, ensuring abundant harvests. So seriously did she take her work that she neglected to care for herself. Call on Pomona when issues of abundance, or lack thereof, are at stake, or when you need a reminder to tend to yourself as carefully as you do those around you.

Rosmerta (Celtic) This powerful goddess of abundance, fertility, prosperity, and well-being was known as the Great Provider. She carried an overflowing basket of fruit or cornucopia, telling us of her generous nature and role as provider of prosperity. She is often depicted with a butter churn, thought to be symbolic of abundance, nourishment, and transformation, in the same way as the Celtic cauldron. Call on Rosmerta to provide a fruitful harvest in whatever activities you're invested.

Snotra (Norse) Snotra is goddess of learning, wisdom, and hospitality, and especially of customs, courtesies, and manners. Snotra can be especially helpful at any gathering where people may not know each other. Mark the Sabbat celebration of Mabon to honor Snotra.

The Horai/Horae (Greek) Goddesses of order and the cyclical nature of the four seasons, the Horai were joyous in spirit and elegantly adorned with flowers and fruits. Coordinate your intentions with the seasons and the bountiful treasures of each when working with the Horai.

YOUR KITCHEN GODDESS POWER

You, kitchen goddess, have as much power as any goddess discussed here. For what is more magical than birthing, raising, and tending to others and making them feel loved and seen? Than showing up every day to feed, nourish, nurture, and support others who depend on you? Than sharing your soul and wisdom? Than caring for Earth?

Whether your kitchen witch journey is just beginning or fully realized, your magic continues to grow the more you use it and the more you share it. Let Nature be your guide but know your true power lies in believing and trusting in your abilities and listening to their pull, intuition, and messages. Each kitchen goddess is in charge of her own realm. So, don't compare yourself to others, but do look to them for inspiration and learning. Your magic is yours to use to make a difference in the world. As above, so below.

The English Alewife

Evidence suggests beer making dates back to circa 4000 BCE and that beer has been a beverage of choice since then. Its origins are credited to the Sumerians—it was the Sumerian women, after all, who brewed the beer; they even had a beer goddess, Ninkasi, whom they worshipped for this great gift. Through civilizations, this gift of the goddess, and oftentimes gods, continued to be highly valued—sometimes even serving as payment for work instead of money.

Beer brewing in its simplest form is a way to preserve fall's grain harvest for consumption throughout the winter, and since the kitchen, and the foods prepared within it, was historically the domain of the women of the house, beer making was also within their bailiwick. And so it followed that the first official brew masters were women—called "brewsters"—and as such, the industrious alewife, and all her ancestors before her, is a prime example of kitchen witchery and a kitchen goddess in action.

As an important source of calories from protein, carbohydrates, and other nutrients, beer was consumed by the entire family. It was an important staple in the household and a significant responsibility for the maker.

In the Middle Ages, beer was flavored with a mix of herbs that were also valued for their magical and medicinal properties, which transitioned to hops. In colonial America, colonists made beer from anything they grew, from corn to tomatoes to pumpkin. They used tree bark, spices, maple sap, fruits, and even flowers to flavor their concoctions. Beer making also uses yeast, a common ingredient in kitchen magic that gives us our daily bread, and other flavorings regularly tossed into the pot on the hearth. And as beer was made from boiled water, deterring disease may have been a secondary benefit.

Some industrious alewives even turned beer making into a moneymaker, selling beer at market or from their homes to supplement income and provide for the family, or helping husbands run the family beer business. Sporting tall hats, often black (it was the fashion) and often pointed (again, the fashion), so as to be seen in the crowd, the beer-selling alewife was easily spotted. If selling from her home, a broomstick placed near the door signaled "open for business," and cats nearby kept mice away. Tending the bubbling cauldron holding her secret brew, her association with today's image of a witch is striking, though not entirely reliable.

However, these clever and courageous women, having perfected the craft of beer making, then went on to perfect their business of selling the brew, and the men of the market took notice—and were decidedly unhappy about the trend. In an attempt to right the imbalance of women in the workplace, a place they shouldn't have been at the time (!), people circulated rumors and stories that these broom-wielding, cauldron-tending, cat-fancying, brew-making sorcerers were, in fact, witches, and their brews were poisoned or hexed. And, at that time in history and for many reasons, witches were not tolerated and even highly feared, so the results were dramatic. At the least, a loss of business; at the worst, jail, even death.

Although the males took over the business of beer making, and still today dominate the industry begun by creative females, women have been entering the craft beer business in growing numbers, a sort of returning to their original beer-making roots, if you will. Cheers!

BREWING MAGIC

Brews don't have to be just ales. Brewed tea, whether made from true tea leaves of the plant *Camellia sinensis* or herbal tea, which is technically a tisane—an infusion brewed with any edible plant part, such as leaves, seeds, bark, blossoms, and roots—has a long history of use the world over for health, healing, and spiritual purposes, dating back to ancient China and Egypt. And the spiritually soothing ritual of preparing and sipping a cup of tea is observed in many cultures.

In addition to the bodily nourishment it provides, tea can nurture the mind and soul. Simply holding the warm cup in your hands and inhaling the soothing aroma can provide an instant feeling of well-being.

Herbs and tea leaves carry with them the energies derived from the soil in which they were grown, the water that nurtured them, and the unique vibrational energies and healing properties in their essence. When combined with the healing, soothing properties of water (especially Moon water), a cup of tea is a magical balm.

Whether you choose to purchase your teas or use fresh herbs from your kitchen garden (those gathered under the Moon's light will be even more inspiring), select a single herb or blend based on intention. As the tea steeps, close your eyes and inhale the aromas while you meditate, even if for just a few seconds, on what you wish to influence. Sweeten with dried fruits, spices, or honey, as desired. All outcomes must be for the good, or your tea will be used in vain.

Divination—It's in the Leaves

In addition to their healing, soothing, refreshing, and energizing properties, tea leaves (maybe more importantly) hold the mysteries of life.

Reading tea leaves, called tasseomancy, to divine your fortune has been practiced for centuries. It's a form of divination, predicting the future, based on interpreting the symbols formed from the tea leaves remaining in a cup after it's been drained.

Reading tea leaves relies on intuition and observation. As with all forms of magic, reading tea leaves takes practice, but it's something anyone can do. It's also a chance to incorporate a mini ritual into your day that can be grounding as well as magical, and to enjoy a cup of tea with a little fun.

Tools needed are simple: Gather a favorite teacup with a saucer (a white-colored cup and saucer is best so the leaves are easily visible, but don't use a mug—you need the sloping sides of the cup and wide rim for best results), a broad-leafed black, green, or white loose tea, just not from a teabag (Darjeeling, jasmine, and Earl Grey are good choices), a teaspoon, and boiling water.

In your cup, combine a scant teaspoon of loose tea leaves with boiling water to fill the cup. Let brew for 3 to 5 minutes. You can add honey or lemon, but no milk. Sip your tea slowly while you relax and let the magic of the tea's warmth and aroma soothe you while your energy infuses the liquid. Use the time to meditate on any questions you have or issues you're facing. When you have just a sip of liquid left in the cup, swirl it three times, counterclockwise, then gently tip the cup upside down into the saucer to drain the liquid. Tap the bottom of the cup three times, turn the cup right side up, and hold it in front of you, near your heart with the handle pointing toward your body, to reveal the secrets within.

The Key *to* Your Cup—
Past, Present, Future

The handle is like home base, representing you. It's where you begin the reading. The nearer the symbols are to the handle, the nearer they are to appearing in your life. Likewise, symbols at the bottom of the cup represent the distant future, and symbols at the sides of the cup are not far into the future.

Let your mind work freely as you examine the shapes and symbols. Imagine finding shapes in the clouds on a warm summer's day. What shapes are represented by the leaves themselves? Or formed by the leaves together? Or in the white space between the leaves? The shapes may be more suggestive than literal; let your intuition have free rein. Pay attention to size, too. The larger the image, the more important or intense the message. Starting at the handle and working clockwise around the cup from the rim to the bottom, make a list, then jot down what the symbols mean to you.

The Ritual *of* Reading Tea Leaves

To be fully prepared and present for reading tea leaves, whether for yourself or someone else, follow these simple steps:

1. Create a calm environment with no distractions where you can focus.

2. Start with a clean cup to ensure the energy it contains is not left over or contaminated.

3. While boiling the water and brewing the tea, meditate on the question you'd like answered or the problem you're yearning to solve.

4. While drinking the tea, don't rush . . . let the tea's taste and aroma gently calm and center you. Feel yourself relax and stress melt away.

5. Keep an open mind. The symbols can have many meanings. Your intuition will guide you as to the story they're meant to tell.

6. Let your subconscious work on the meanings if they're not immediately clear to you and leave judgment at the door.

7. End the reading with a moment of gratitude for all that life has given you.

A PRIMER FOR READING TEA LEAVES

If you discern the following shapes in your tea leaves, translate them with this simple key, and let your intuition guide you. Some shapes can have obvious meanings, like a heart for love, or an initial for a past or future lover or friend. Relate the shapes and meanings to your life, or the life of whoever you're reading for, to reveal what the leaves may be telling you for a more personal interpretation. And note: The tea leaves only work their magic for good. Though life has its ups and downs, the leaves can warn but they will not harm. No evil will be found at the bottom of any teacup.

Acorn: health, strength, and gain through hard work; good fortune awaits if several acorns appear

Anchor: good and loyal friends, success in business, manifestation of your dreams

Angel: good fortune in love; happiness and peace, protection

Apple: long life

Bell: news

Birds: happiness and joy, travel

Bones: overcoming misfortune with great courage

Book: if open, you're open to new information; closed, an indication of secrets

Bouquet: future happiness, love, fulfilled hope, marriage

Broom: a warning to choose friends wisely and be wary of rushing into new relationships, fresh starts

 **Butterfly:** intuition, transformation

Candle: hope in darkness

Cat: independence, trickery

Cauldron: new opportunities that need careful consideration

Circle: an engagement, faithful friends, money

Clouds: trouble

Cross: obstacles in the way of your desires

Dog: friendship and loyalty

Dragon: unexpected change, perhaps revealing opportunity

Eggs: new plans and ideas, or a birth

Fish: news from abroad; things are going "swimmingly"

Heart: love

Horseshoe: unexpected good fortune

Hourglass: time is running out to accomplish your plans

House: a new home

Initials: suggestive of names of people or places

Knife: danger

Ladder: travel

Lion: a most fortunate signal of honor and fame

Moon: success and happiness; a crescent moon denotes fortune

Mushroom: expect great success from a small risk; or, a quarrel among lovers

Parallel lines: expect plans to go smoothly

Shamrock: good luck

Snake: disloyalty, hidden danger, treachery

Square: comfort and peace

Star: a symbol of luck; if surrounded by dots, wealth and honor are forthcoming

Tree: happiness, good health, prosperity

Triangle: a fortunate encounter

Unicorn: scandal

Urn: illness

Wheel: progress, or forthcoming inheritance

The KITCHEN WITCH & the MOON

Witches of all types love the Moon and it should have no less importance than the Sun. For many, the Moon was the first calendar that guided planting and harvesting of foods that sustained life. If you're a kitchen witch with a kitchen garden, you're likely already attuned to the Moon and her phases.

The ritual of mealtime brings lots of opportunity to stir up some magic in our lives. Using the Moon's guidance as another ingredient in your kitchen magic arsenal can be a way to boost your magical intuition and your magical living, as well as inspire new ways of looking at life.

The Moon's Magic

The idea of the Moon as magical stems from the idea that the Moon's phases, as well as the waxing and waning of life itself, are all interconnected. The Moon's changing phases mean her energies, too, wax and wane over the course of her monthly journey through our skies, affecting not only our tides on Earth, but also the tides of our emotions and moods. Whether you choose to be in tune with the Moon and her magic in your kitchen through all of her phases each month; mark just the beginning, middle, and end phases with intention; or channel the power and pleasure of each Full Moon is entirely up to you. Follow your intuition.

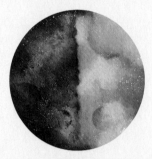

NEW MOON

Beginning of the cycle and a time
of cleansing; an active phase, a
time to set intentions, plan new
beginnings, make new resolutions.

FIRST QUARTER MOON

Stronger light brings focus to
intentions. In this active phase, if
you have not already done so, take
appropriate actions to realize your
intentions as energies build.

WAXING CRESCENT MOON

Growing light offers a clearer glimpse
of your intentions. This reflective
phase is a time to refine intentions
and consider the actions needed to
manifest them.

WAXING GIBBOUS MOON

Building excitement nurtures hopes
and dreams. In this reflective phase,
trust that your actions are aligned
with your intentions.

FULL MOON

This is the time of highest energy, abundance, fruition, and gratitude. It can also be a time of letting go. This is an active phase, so assess results, celebrate achievements, and offer gratitude for abundance.

LAST (THIRD) QUARTER MOON

Acknowledge what went well, what didn't go as planned, and the hard work you've committed to living your best life. This is an active phase, so let go of guilt or judgment or anything that is not a positive force in your life; indulge in self-care to recharge your batteries. Forgive yourself and others.

WANING GIBBOUS MOON

This reflective phase is a time to meditate on lessons learned. Consider where you've grown, request feedback, share your story, and recognize what no longer serves.

WANING CRESCENT MOON

The cycle ends and darkness signals a time to rest and reflect inward on priorities; appreciate the quiet so you can hear your soul talking as you prepare for the beginning of a new cycle.

KITCHEN MAGIC & MOON MAGIC:
A LOVELY RECIPE

Planting and harvesting with the Moon's phases as a guide has been practiced throughout history. For the kitchen witch who also selects and prepares foods with the phases, it is the chance to multiply the Moon's power into one amazing boost to your magic. Thoughtfully cooking and eating with the Moon's phases offers another tool to live "seasonally"— following the seasons of the Moon, and her lead to go with the flow. And, being that much more aware of the intentions behind what you eat serves as a reminder of the goals you're working to manifest, and nourishes your intentions more purposefully.

NEW MOON

As a time of new beginnings, explore new foods or unfamiliar cuisines, try new recipes, or designate the time to meditate on how freshness can enhance your life. As a time of darkness and cleansing, you'll naturally be drawn to lighter meals. Bitter foods, such as lemon, radicchio, arugula, and dandelion greens, cleanse the body and spirit. Turmeric, asparagus, avocado, and artichoke are great detoxifiers as well. As the darkness gives way to light, try some herbs for inspiration and motivation, such as lemon verbena, lemon thyme, ginger, or peppermint. Lots of water is important, too—try Moon water flavored with lemon or cucumber.

WAXING MOON PHASES (WAXING CRESCENT, FIRST QUARTER, WAXING GIBBOUS)

At the start of these phases, the Moon's light is in its infancy. Connect with childhood memories and recreate some favorite family meals or treats, or scour those forgotten seed catalogs to map out your kitchen garden. This is a time of nurturing and growing excitement—plan a party or gathering to increase the vibrations even more.

As energies build in the sky, so, too, do they below as activity picks up in working your plans. Spicy foods that energize and excite are prime candidates—think big, bold flavors for big, bold ideas and actions—as well as foods that make you feel nourished, strong, and excited. Lots of protein from legumes, such as edamame, peas, beans, and peanuts, as well as almonds, quinoa, broccoli, and dark leafy greens will keep you on track. Protective foods that will keep you healthy, like onion and garlic, should be used liberally. Season with herbs, such as rosemary, thyme, ginseng, or basil, to clear the mind (and cobwebs), nourish, and restore so you may focus on the job at hand. Share your light and spirit to help others who are struggling. Consider donating to a food pantry.

FULL MOON

This celebratory time recognizes achievements and should be savored. Bring on the feasts and special treats as rewards for your hard work. Dish up the carbs, as you'll need the energy, and chocolate is without doubt required. Most definitely, fill your cauldron with fresh water, set it under the Full Moon's glow, and ask for her blessing. Use your Moon water, then, for cooking, drinking, bathing, or brewing a cup of tea and divining your future (see page 39). And though a time of emotional highs, a bit of grounding can keep us real. Try cabbage, rutabaga, beets, kiwi, and salt to stay steeped in reality. Flavor foods liberally with fresh herbs to kick-start that celebratory feel.

WANING MOON PHASES (WANING GIBBOUS, THIRD QUARTER, WANING CRESCENT)

The deepening darkness of these final phases signals a time to rest, relax, and reflect. Order takeout (intentionally, of course) so someone else does the cooking tonight! Or, break out that special bottle of wine or box of chocolates you've been saving for something special. You're special.

Clean out the pantry and refrigerator so your tools remain fresh, relevant, and meaningful. Accept change as it comes your way.

Cozy foods, like soups and casseroles, have that vibe, especially when they incorporate relaxing herbs to help you slow down, open your mind and heart, and boost your intuition so you're receptive to Nature's messages and signals.

This is also a time of forgiveness. Try basil, lavender, lemongrass, or ginger, or a brew of St. John's wort. In the spirit of caring for Earth, embrace leftovers to minimize waste and show gratitude for your bounty.

ESBAT

The energies of Esbat correspond to the energies of the Moon's eight phases, but because there are eight phases *each month*, many mark Esbat with the Full Moon and, sometimes, New Moon.

Celebrating Esbat at the New Moon offers a chance for introspection and self-reflection; the extra-magical Full Moon reveals a full-on celebration, which also includes the symbolic Cakes and Ale ritual, a sharing of food and drink in honor of the Moon as Mother Goddess and giver of all things. The "cake" can be anything from bread to cookies, crackers, muffins, or actual cake, and is offered with a blessing, such as "may you never feel hunger." The "ale" is next, and can be any liquid you like, or influenced by the season. Examples include lemonade in summer, cider in fall, or Champagne if celebrating a special occasion. Pair your drink with a blessing, too, such as "may you never thirst."

However you celebrate, cast your magic for the good of all and with a healthy dose of gratitude.

The MAGIC of the KITCHEN GARDEN

An extension of the kitchen, really, this special plot of land, often just steps from the home and used to grow food to feed the family, has historically been tended by the women in the household for as long as there has been a division of labor. Of course, anyone can tend this garden, but it is an especially powerful place for the kitchen witch—a magical space where you can be inspired, set intentions, harvest, and manifest, full of nourishing fruits and vegetables, healing herbs, sacred trees, and secrets to a fulfilling life. There is much magic to be discovered here each season.

The kitchen garden's success depends some on luck and weather and lots on careful planning and tending. Each seed planted represents a seed of intention, growing to nourish, heal, and delight. With proper and successive plantings as well as harvesting and preserving, a modest kitchen garden can feed the family for much of the year, offering the surprise of something different every day—with little wasted.

Today's Magical Kitchen Garden

Today's kitchen garden is just as likely to be a 9 × 12-foot (270 × 360 cm) plot as it is a windowsill pot or patio raised bed. If space is an issue, use pots, or create a themed garden, such as a tea garden. Farmers' markets are ideal replacements if you've no room to grow your own plants. Grocery stores are fine, too, but freshness may be compromised during the time it takes to get food to the store and into your home. As the kitchen witch who tends a garden knows, seasonality is key—so buy what's in season for the freshest, most magical ingredients.

A kitchen garden is also a reminder of all we're working to manifest in life. It's a sanctuary where you can escape the noise and commune with Nature's emissaries, even if only for a few minutes a day. There, you'll find a sense of peace, calm, and accomplishment. Tending Earth soothes the soul and calms the mind, and provides much-needed meditative time, time to be fully absorbed in the task at hand and feel connected in a primal way to the Universe. Immersing your hands and feet in the Earth's soil transfers her grounding energy to you. The elements and Spirit are all present and prove valuable allies in this task. And seeds gathered, sown, and reaped under a Full Moon bring their own energy to the cauldron. Senses become fully engaged and being present in the moment is a reward in and of itself.

Lots of vegetables and fruits are covered in this book (see The Wheel of the Year, page 66), so incorporate your favorites into any themed herbal garden suggestions. As you tend your garden, breathe in its scents and breathe out any worry or negativity. Your magic, and your magical garden, will be thriving in no time.

MAGICALLY THEMED HERBAL GARDENS

Fresh herbs are Nature's little miracles. They add flavor to food, scents to bouquets, magic to intentions, and substance to spellwork. In our magical apothecary, "herbs" include all types of plants, including traditional herbs, spices, flowers, and trees—all with the potential to promote soothing, bewitchery, and charm. Be sure to note, *not all herbs wield their magic as edible plants.* Some cast their spell with scent, color, beauty, or texture. Do your research when planting and harvesting to know what's safe to consume, including knowing any contraindications for your circumstances, or what should just be used as a symbol of your intentions.

And herbs' magic is not restricted to one thing or issue. So, tuck them into a wreath based on intentions set, or sprinkle them in food to tend to your family's well-being. Sip a cuppa to entice what you desire, garnish a cocktail to boost its vibrations, or season gifts to share the magic of your kitchen.

Growing herbs is relatively easy. If space or time is an issue, or you're a beginner, a small herbal garden can be an ideal way to reap the bounty without a big commitment. You don't need a plot of land, just some pots, seeds, soil, water, and sunshine—inside or out—plus a few tools and a spell for abundance! And, if growing your own is not in the cards, stock your herbal apothecary with what you find at the grocers' or farmers' market.

Some theme ideas are presented here to get you started. Your themes can also be built around specific foods or cuisines, like a pizza garden, salad garden, pesto garden, soup garden, or Mediterranean garden.

ALL-PURPOSE KITCHEN HERB GARDEN

Basil: courage, good wishes, love, wealth

Chamomile: comfort, patience, sleep

Chives: breaking bad habits, guarding against harmful spirits

Cilantro: money magic

Comfrey: repels ghosts, safe travel

Dandelion: wishes granted

Echinacea: inner strength

Fennel: flattery, praiseworthy

Fern: boosts the magical energy of other herbs (Note: **Most ferns are not edible.**)

Lavender: cleansing, devotion, peace

Lemon balm: family harmony, sympathy

Mint: increases the power of our words, refreshment, travel

Nasturtium: fosters creativity, releases fears

Oregano: protects the home from evil influences; tranquility, vitality

Parsley: celebration, gratitude

Rosemary: clarity, remembrance

Sage: longevity, wisdom

Thyme: affection and loyalty; courage

Vervain, a.k.a. the enchanter's herb: clear communication, protection from evil spells, purification

HEALING GARDEN

Allspice: energy, healing, luck, virility

Aloe vera: beauty, healing, protection, luck (Note: Aloe's

magic is in the soothing gel contained within the leaves. **It is generally not edible.**)

Angelica: wards off ills

Caraway: fortifies health and spirit to weather any storm

Chamomile: soothes a troubled spirit

Chives: guards against illness

Cilantro: supports health and healing

Elderberry: helps ease colds and flu

Feverfew (leaf): eases aches and pains, especially of aging

Ginger: boosts immunity

Sage: eases grief

St. John's wort: brightens mood

Yarrow: strong in healing spells

LOVE GARDEN

Apple blossom: beauty, fertility, joyful love

Basil: fidelity in love, forgiveness

Cardamom: aphrodisiac to some, charm, relaxation

Cilantro: promotes love and lust

Clover: protects friendships

Garlic: aphrodisiac, passion, strength (and repels the odd vampire or two)

Oregano: add to love potions

 Rose: speaks the language of love

Spearmint: compassion, love, wisdom

Viola: faithful companionship

MONEY GARDEN

Allspice: for growing your fortune and increasing luck

Basil: especially holy basil (tulsi), said to carry the good fortune of the goddess Lakshmi

Bay leaf: success

Bergamot: breeds success, which bestows money

Ginger: protects against poverty, attracts new opportunities

Lady's mantle: beads of dew that form on the leaves are said to transform metal into gold

Marjoram: show me the money!

Nutmeg: tuck into your shoe for luck when gambling

Patchouli: attracts money and abundance (Note: The magic is in the plant's calming scent. **It is not edible.**)

Thyme: brings money into the home

MOON GARDEN

Jasmine: reveals beauty in all things (Note: The magic is within this plant's glorious scent. **It is not edible.**)

Lamb's ear: enhances listening and understanding; healing wounds both physical and spiritual (Note: The magic is in this plant's soothing texture, and the benefit to pollinators in your garden. **It is not edible.**)

Lavender: calm

Moonflower: divination, dreams, intuition (Note: This plant conjures magic with its moody vibe and night-blooming flowers. **It is not edible.**)

Moonwort: encourages honesty, promises prosperity, repels monsters

Sage: grants wisdom and wishes

White bleeding heart: heals grief, opens aching hearts to new love (Note: Let its beauty enchant you. **It is not edible.**)

White coneflower: inner strength, protection

White sweet alyssum: calming energy, protection against deception, the evil eye, and insanity

Wooly thyme: creates a magical carpet for the fairies to dance upon (Note: **It is not edible or suitable for culinary use.**)

STRENGTH AND PROTECTION GARDEN

Angelica: prophetic visions, protection

Bay leaf: glory, strength, success

Dill: luck, protection from evil

Fern: protection from evil witches (Note: **Most ferns are not edible.**)

Garlic: protects health, property, and wealth

Marsh mallow: especially protective of children

Mugwort: able to drive away demons

Tansy: reverses any spells cast your way (Note: **This plant is poisonous. Do not consume.**)

Tarragon: inspires courage and confidence

Thyme: courage

TEA GARDEN

Basil (leaves): love, money spells, protection

Chamomile (blossoms): comfort, patience, sleep

Echinacea (blossoms): immunity; inner strength

Hibiscus flower (blossoms): attracts love, intuition, Moon magic

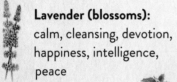

Lavender (blossoms): calm, cleansing, devotion, happiness, intelligence, peace

Lemon balm (leaves): sympathy

Lemon thyme, common thyme (leaves and sprigs): beauty, courage, good health, prevents nightmares, protection, removes negative energy, sleep

Lemon verbena (leaves and blossoms): inspiration

Mint (leaves): clear and meaningful communication, refreshment, travel

Passion flower (leaves): hospitality, relaxation, soothes strong emotions

Rose (hips, spent blooms): immunity boost, love

Rosemary (leaves): clarity, purification, remembrance, sweet dreams

St. John's wort (blossoms): eases depression, promotes serenity

WITCH'S GARDEN

Use the herbs of the witch's garden wisely, for their magic is powerful. They are best used as stand-ins for your intentions and manifesting desired outcomes. They are not suggested for culinary use or recommended as edible.

Buttercup, a.k.a. toe of frog: hold one under the chin—a yellow reflection indicates the truth is being told; add to attract fairy companions, or bring luck and prosperity

 Catnip: attracts luck, for beauty, cat magic

Coltsfoot, a.k.a. horse's hoof: divination, love spells, money spells, springtime rituals

Comfrey, a.k.a. ear of ass: protection for travelers

Dandelion leaves, a.k.a. pig's snout: divination, persistence

False unicorn root, a.k.a. unicorn's horn: fertility

Foxglove, a.k.a. bloody fingers or witch's bells: protection (Note: **Poisonous. Do not consume.**)

Houndstongue, a.k.a. tongue of dog: increases the ability to blend intellect and intuition for clear decisions

Moonflower: spirit communication

Moss, a.k.a. wool of bat: luck, protection against evil spirits

Mustard seed, a.k.a. eye of newt:  black mustard seeds bestow fertility, mental acuity, protection, success with court cases; yellow mustard seeds counter negative energies and bring luck and love

Parsley: rumored to grow profusely when grown from seed by true witches

Witch hazel: protection

The Magic of Trees

Trees, of course, are magical beings, too. If you have room for them in your kitchen garden, they are a blessing and can be powerful allies in your magical work. If not, visualize the tree and its magical properties as you set intentions or cast spells. Use a tree's offerings, such as fallen nuts, pine cones, leaves, twigs, fruit, or flowers, on your kitchen altar, in spellwork, and for goddess offerings. Get to know the trees in your neighborhood. When you "meet" in real life, give the tree a hug . . . you'll feel its heartbeat and energy fill you with joy.

Birch: "the wood of choice" for witches' brooms; new beginnings; cleansing

Ash: wide-reaching magical reputation from water spells to spells for protection, health, prosperity, love, and prophetic intuition; a favorite wood for Druids' wands

Banyan: Hindus believe this is the Tree of Life, able to make wishes come true and attract wealth, luck, and abundance to you

Dogwood: durability, protection, trust

Elder: called "the tree of music" by some; its branches make lovely recorders, flutes, and whistles—a favorite of the music-making fairy kingdom; it is said that to sleep under the elder is to dance among the fairies

Oak: home to the magical mistletoe (see page 113)

Pine: adaptability, cleansing, grounding, immortality

Hawthorn: the legendary tree of the fairies—a place so sacred, grave harm may befall any who deface it. Portals to magical realms are said to exist beneath the flowering hawthorn

Rowan: plant next to the home for the most protection from evil spirits

Hazel: these delightful nuts are a favorite among garden fairies

Willow: healing, inner vision and dreams, learning, loyalty, trust

Edible Flowers

Many beautiful herbal and floral blooms, in addition to the magic they carry, are edible and provide the opportunity to add a bit of glamour and beauty to your kitchen magic. They add even more meaning when used beyond their eye appeal, to work a little magic into your meal or send sweet messages to those for whom you cook and love. Add them to salads, cakes, cookies, platters and boards, cocktails, mocktails, ice cubes, and anything else you can think of. Flavors range from mild and sweet to floral, minty, herbal, garlicky, and peppery.

A word of caution: Edible flowers should only be consumed when you know precisely what the flower is, that it is edible, and that it was grown organically, without chemicals. If you have allergies, use for decorative purposes only. Growing your own edible flowers ensures you know what you have and allows you to set intentions with them from the moment you plant the seeds.

Bee balm: friendship, lucid dreams, success

Begonia: protection and watchful warnings

Apple blossom: variously a symbol of immortality, of the dead, of health and vitality, and of preference

Bachelor button: blessings

Chamomile: calm, healing, and loving protection

Chive blossom: love, protection, purpose

Pansy: charm

Rose petals: love and passion

Dandelion: abundance, adaptation, intuition, wishes granted

Dianthus: true love

Lavender: dispelling fear, serenity

Squash blossom: balance, success, vitality

Lilac: a ghost buster for sure; a fairy favorite for its joyful and lucky energies

Sunflower: happiness, personal growth, truth

Marigold: money, protection from evil, a sunny disposition

Nasturtium: victory

Violet: honor, intuition, loyalty; also a fairy magnet

PART 2

The
WHEEL
of the
YEAR

Attributed to the ancient Celts, the Wheel of the Year is a calendar that tracks the turn of the seasons and the flow of life, marking them at time-honored points celebrating the Sun as well as Earth and her bounty, but with room for personal rituals and magical gatherings along the way.

As seasonality and the transformation it brings are the creed of the kitchen witch, attuning your craft to the seasons is a must, for each brings a time and purpose to your work as well as a guiding energy to your life. Embrace the message.

The Wheel of the Year comprises eight Sabbat celebrations—four corresponding to the Sun's solstices and equinoxes, and four to the seasons and their harvests. Their lesson is gratitude: to acknowledge and be thankful for all that's been given as well as remember and honor what's been lost, a way of keeping life in balance.

Not technically part of the "Wheel" (though some call it a second Wheel of the Year) but a part of magical living no less, woven between the Sabbats are Esbat celebrations (see page 50), which provide another opportunity to give thanks and manifest intentions.

Using seasonal recipes, celebrations, rituals, foods, recipes, and spells, blending magic born of Earth and transformed in your kitchen into everyday life enhances your connection and communication with Nature, honors Earth in a positive and sustainable way, and transforms magical energy into intention and intention into manifestation.

As the Wheel turns, the seasons dance to their own rhythm. Let the seasons lead you but make the dance yours. The powers of Earth are the tools of your magical kitchen and the secrets of every kitchen witch everywhere. Savor the endless possibilities.

FALL

Though this season on the Wheel of the Year marks the harvest's end and a time for Earth to rest and renew, it's also the time when Samhain occurs, which marks the beginning of the witch's new year and the Wheel of the Year, so here we'll start our journey.

Attuned to Nature and its language, the kitchen witch senses that, as the temperatures decrease and the days grow shorter, Earth signals that it's time to gather the last harvest and prepare for rest. She also knows that before rest, though, comes the work of the harvest and the celebration of its plenty. The autumnal equinox, about September 22 in the Northern Hemisphere (March 20 or 21 in the Southern) marks the beginning of the season, which lasts until winter solstice (see page 109).

As though she knows of the celebrations in store, Earth puts on one of her most colorfully dazzling displays, lifting the spirits and begging you to join the dance. The crops harvested now tend to be a bit sturdier in personality, with strong grounding energies and persevering characteristics that help them stay viable over winter to continue to nourish us, as we reap the rewards that magical living affords.

A FALL
Blessing

May the blessings of fall feed the wisdom of my soul and teach my spirit gratitude for each gift.

May the hearth fires warm those who gather nearby and speak "welcome" to those who return.

For the plenty that sustains us through winter's dark times I give thanks.

MABON

The name "Mabon" comes to us from Welsh mythology, telling of a handsome young god named Mabon who had been held captive in the Underworld as a baby. The pagan celebration and Wiccan Sabbat of Mabon, generally September 21 (about March 21 in the Southern Hemisphere), corresponds with the autumnal equinox and is one of four festivals during the Wheel of the Year celebrating the harvest.

With this equinox comes a balance in our lives: the times of daylight and darkness, or yin and yang, are equal; we simultaneously celebrate the life-giving qualities of Earth, yet also acknowledge and plan for the darker times ahead—life turns to death, yet we anticipate rebirth; a time of hellos and good-byes. It's also a time of thanksgiving, for a successful crop (be that whatever you're tending: gardens, families, careers, talents, friendships, or relationships), fattened animals, and manifestation of plans carefully tended to sustain us through winter. It is space in our lives that makes real the idea of committing to see intentions through to fruition and the idea that we can manifest the life we choose. It is a time of transition and transformation.

It is also a time of reflection and letting go of what no longer serves and of grieving what was lost, so our coming period of rest may be tranquil and restorative.

If you're not quite ready for the harvest, that's okay: Remember, what stays on the vine of intentions only grows sweeter and riper. Don't wait too long, though, to tend to your crops, or they may be lost.

For the kitchen witch, the flavors of Mabon are long-simmering, cozy, and warm; the energies joyous, grounding, and hopeful. A time of plenty, the traditional symbol of Mabon is the overflowing cornucopia, as well as the nuts and seeds, and apple and grapes.

CELEBRATING MABON

There are as many ways to celebrate Mabon as there are revelers. A list of favorites follows. Give them a try or mull on the suggestions to conjure rituals and activities to make it your own and express your gratitude.

- Go apple picking—then transform those glorious apples into all kinds of tasty treats (such as Love Charm Apple Butter, page 91).

- Invite other kitchen witches to a harvest celebration, gather in a circle to amplify the energy, and toast to your bounty.

- Decorate your kitchen altar in colors of red, gold, and brown.

- Take a walk and breathe in fall's energizing aromas.

- Meditate on the word "balance" and explore the insight you get.

- Fashion a besom broom for a ceremonial clearing of the cobwebs.

- Decorate your porch with cornstalks and pumpkins.

- Light a fire in your hearth, or a candle on your tabletop, for its cozy warmth.

- Drink wine (responsibly).

- Practice the yoga Tree pose for balance . . . with eyes closed for an extra challenge.

- Host a thanksgiving celebration meal to share your gratitude.

- Preserve the abundance of foods from your garden (or from your local farmers' market) and share them with others as a way to bring joy and sustain relationships.

- Journal about all the things you're grateful for.

- Feed the birds.

- Consult your tarot deck.

Besom Broom Ritual *for* Cleansing *and* Protection

The broom is an ancient tool that holds magical roots, with many believing in its powers to sweep away the bad as well as past evils that still haunt.

When one thinks "broom," one often thinks "witch," and the besom broom is one of the most-associated symbols of witches and witchcraft and is also one of the earliest types of broom known. These brooms were often hung, bristles up, near doorways to guard against evil entering a home and to protect all inside. It will sweep in good luck. It is also a symbolic cleansing tool used to clear away any negative energies when preparing for spellwork, whether that's in reference to people or vibes.

Mabon and Samhain are optimal times for bringing out the besom—to clear away the old and make way for the new, as well as protecting from rogue spirits. You can make your own besom broom (there are lots of tutorials online) or buy one if you prefer. Perform this simple ritual to mark your intention.

Take a moment to breathe deeply to cleanse yourself of any negative thoughts, feelings, or energies. Visualize what you desire to manifest in the new year and, when ready, say quietly or aloud:

I charge this broom to sweep away the dust and dirt that block my way,
To signal ghosts just passing by, there's nothing here for you to spy.
As what is old is swept away, I see the space to grow take shape.
For what has been did serve to teach, expand my views, extend my reach.
With gratitude I clear the way for magic to infuse my days.

Then, sweep all the rooms in your home with your household broom—paying special attention to the kitchen—to clear away dust, debris, and anything negatively invading your space. Sweep your porch and walkway clear as well, as you give thanks for what was and visualize what you desire to manifest in the new year.

Gather your besom and symbolically sweep your altar (if you have one) and kitchen, since that's the prime spot for your magical craft. You can spritz a little cleansing spray while doing this, if you wish (sage, lemon, or pine would be perfect).

Hang the besom—bristles up, remember—near a doorway for luck and protection, until needed next.

So mote it be.

SAMHAIN

One of the most important of the Sabbat festivals, usually October 31 in the Northern Hemisphere (April 30 in the Southern Hemisphere), Samhain marks the beginning of the Wheel of the Year and signifies the witch's new year, also known today as Halloween or All Hallows' Eve, and marks the start of the dark half of the year. The darkness symbolizes rest, but also the excitement of the unknown and unseen as we step into this new year of the Wheel. And for the kitchen witch looking to divine a little intel on what the new year may hold, gather the most sacred of Samhain's harvest foods, the hazelnut, and be sure to eat a few before sitting with your crystal ball or teacup.

The traditional symbol of the holiday is the jack-o'-lantern, which arose, as many tales tell, when a crafty old Irish fellow named Stingy Jack tricked the Devil into buying him a drink—to Jack's delight and the Devil's furious despair. And, for reasons unknown, Jack gets away with it again!—and is then banished from both Heaven and Hell by the irate Devil. Poor Jack wanders restlessly through his remaining days (and nights) with only a lowly carved turnip, in which sits a lit coal, for guidance. The rest, as they say, is history.

Samhain celebrations, historically lasting three days and three nights, honor the last harvest of the year, and are associated with fire, with great bonfires representing the Sun—with a dual purpose to help warn away evil spirits—traditionally part of the festivities. After the celebrations, the home's hearth fire was relit from a torch carried from the bonfire to give warmth and protection through the coming winter.

You may notice a shimmering shadow as daylight grows shorter and the veil to the otherworld thins and, according to ancient beliefs, allows the restless souls of the dearly departed to return to walk the Earth. To protect oneself was to dress to resemble the ghosts and goblins you might encounter, in a sort of sympathetic magic ritual, and the hope that they wouldn't recognize you. Fairies are also active and mischief ensues. Don't ignore those impish trick-or-treaters, for they may be fairies in disguise!

Samhain represents a pause, a breath, in the Earth's growing cycle as she prepares to rest and renew. Samhain is also a time to show gratitude for the last harvest given to us by Earth. It is a time to connect with and remember loved ones who have passed and recognize death as a part of life.

For the kitchen witch, the flavors of Samhain mimic Mabon and include rosemary for remembrance and black pepper for protection. Beets are a traditional food for Samhain, so be sure to include some on the menu. The energies are slower, of rest and renewal. It is a time of balance, of celebration and reflection. The traditional symbols of Samhain are many, including the apple, pumpkin, hazelnut, cauldron, and besom.

CELEBRATING SAMHAIN

Though a time of death—of the land, of sunlit days, of those who've passed, of intentions unrealized—Samhain does not need to be a time of gloom. Celebrations of gratitude for all we've been given, tinged with remembrance for what or who may have been lost, are in order. Here are a few suggestions to ignite ideas:

- Bob for apples, an old Samhain tradition in which unmarried people seeking mates carve their name into an apple before dropping it into the tub. Whoever successfully retrieves the apple using their teeth alone is destined to be "the one."

- Tidy up the house, as you tidy up the garden, in preparation for rest.

- Decorate your home in the colors of the season: orange for joy, changing luck, and energy; black for protection and setting boundaries.

- Drink warm cider on a crisp, cool day as an act of self-love.

- Carve a jack-o'-lantern, including a secret sigil underneath its lid for protection, then roast the seeds and eat them in acknowledgment of the abundance in your life.

- Create a luminary along your property to guide lost souls safely by and send wishes of plenty into the world.

- Visit a loved one's grave and leave an offering of their favorite flowers in honor of how they nourished you in life.

- Have a costume party; attend a witch's ball.

- Meditate, then journal on new intentions for the new year.

- Sprinkle pumpkin pie spice on just about anything your heart desires; its main ingredient, cinnamon, offers protection and reminds you of the abundance you have, even on days you don't feel so blessed.

- Have a "silent dinner," setting chairs, places, and favorite foods at the table for loved ones no longer with us, inviting them to join you that you may reconnect and relive their company. Or, leave a chair and a cup of fresh water on the porch as respite for any wandering souls or restless fairies who may pass by.

- Place your besom across a doorway to invite communication from loved ones passed. Leave it there as long as you feel the conversation continuing.

SOUL CAKES

The modern tradition of trick-or-treating seemingly evolved from ancient Samhain customs. One such custom dating back to the Middle Ages, begging for soul cakes on November 2 (later, All Souls Day and typically the third day of Samhain festivities), a tradition called "souling," may be the likeliest culprit. With a bit of an opposing strategy to those aimed at warding off lost and frightful spirits, or restless souls of the deceased, children and peasants went from house to house begging, and singing, for soul cakes (see page 103)—sweetly scented treats, a cross between a scone and a cookie—with the promise of a prayer for the lost, departed souls to be freed from purgatory on their receipt. Legend has it that when no soul cakes were forthcoming, ill fates awaited!

The Magic of Fall's Bounty: Cozy, Colorful, Copious

As fall appears, the Earth turns slowly away from the Sun, temperatures dip, and days grow short. It is a busy time to reap the last harvest, celebrate its success, and preserve what can be saved for nourishment over winter. It is a time for assessment and reflection and an inward turning of thoughts and activities, a time for sharing your abundance, and lessons learned with others. Mother Earth dons her riotous coat of many colors and the crispness of fall, in her flavors, scents, temperatures, and sounds, crackles with magical possibilities. Let's explore some of fall's most fabulous gifts.

APPLE

Apples, long associated with magic and witchcraft, have the abilities to tempt, heal, and hex. The edible apple blossom indicates preference in the language of flowers; the apple is variously a symbol of immortality, health and vitality (that apple a day!), love, and fertility.

Cut an apple through its core, from the stem end down, and you'll reveal a five-pointed pentagram, in Wicca tradition representing the four natural elements plus Spirit. Once halved, share it with your true love. The blossoms are also five-petaled.

The tradition of polishing an apple before biting into its juicy flesh may endure from times when the rubbing was thought to rid the fruit of any evil hiding inside, a belief likely originating from the apple's association with the temptation of Adam and Eve, and carried forth on the tales of witches using apples to hex and poison their victims.

Apple trees were sacred to the Druids, who believed it was one of only two trees that would support their beloved mistletoe. And the Twelfth Night tradition of wassailing derives from the ancient pagan tradition of singing to the apple trees on this night, hoisting a cheerful mug of wassail to drive away demons and coax an abundant harvest from Earth and her trees in the coming year. The mystical unicorn is said to dwell in the apple orchard—listen for his song.

Apple blossoms and their fruit, full of fiber, vitamins A and C, and quercetin, an antioxidant that may help prevent cancer, are joyous tools to use for healing and love, to bless beauty, boost health and fertility, and spread peace. Apples will fill you with trust and abundance as well.

BANANA

Bananas bring magical energies of fertility, love, and vitality. Feed liberally to potential suitors and await fruitful results. Flowers from the banana plant are sacred in India and bestow good luck on the wearer. Giving bananas to children encourages their independence and a sweet personality.

BEET

The Greek goddess Aphrodite held beets sacred
and used them to maintain her legendary beauty.
Beets promote grounding energies, and can be
used for spells and rituals targeting beauty, love and passion, and long
life; the greens bolster wealth and growth.

BROCCOLI

This mealtime staple is a potent source of antioxidants.
When prepared and eaten with intention, its properties
can promote renewal, protection and strength,
prosperity, and a sense of ease.

BRUSSELS SPROUTS

These tiny cabbage cousins, when enjoyed with a
heart aligned with actions and intentions, inspire
adaptation, protection, grounding, and peace. They
can also reveal hidden layers of communication
when messages seem contradictory.

CABBAGE

Cabbage is protective, in both its mystical energies
and its nutritional benefits. Irish lore holds that a
cabbage plucked under a Full Moon on Halloween
foretells of your future mate: When the roots cling
to the soil, your mate will bring wealth. No soil? Sorry. Now for the
taste: bitter taste equals sour temperament; sweet taste equals happy
marriage. Its color, too, can tell of cabbage's powers: white, like the Full
Moon, boosts spirituality and intuition; red ignites passion for whatever
you need; and green foretells money and growth.

Fall's Spice Pantry

Whether seasoning foods with a boost of flavor or intentions, a well-stocked spice pantry is a kitchen witch's ally in magic. For seasonal fall flavors, these spices are warming, cozy, comforting, and protective. Add your favorites to expand the possibilities.

Black pepper: to counter aggression and regain what's been lost; for adventure, protection, spice, and wealth

 Cardamom: for a clear mind, faithful love, and a sweet temperament

Celery seed: for intuition and potent love potions

 Cinnamon: for love, protection, success, and a boost of magic for manifesting energies

Cloves: eliminates negative energies blocking success; for intuition, love spells, purification, and protection

 Ginger: for healing, love, and warmth

Marjoram: for banishing blues that inevitably arrive as darkness looms; for cleansing and money luck

Nutmeg: for attracting lucky outcomes in games of chance, happy dreams, and soothing the mind

Rosemary: for fidelity, mental clarity, remembrance, and protection from thieves!

Saffron: for happiness; particularly appropriate for any celebrations of the Sun or Sun magic

Sage: for health and long life

Salt: for amplification of messages and meanings, grounding, protection, and wealth (all in moderation)

Sugar: for beauty and love

Turmeric: for cleansing and good health

Vanilla bean: for attracting love

CARROT

The first cultivated carrots, thought to
go back almost five thousand years, were
likely purple, giving them a distinctly royal
vibe. Our old familiar, the orange carrot,

came to be in about the sixteenth century, developed by the Dutch
and subsequently dedicated to Dutch royalty: the House of Orange.
In addition to improving eyesight (including that of your third eye) and
helping slow aging, the (symbolically shaped) carrot can bolster your sex
drive and confidence. Draw out its sweet charms for a beauty boost and
seeing the truth in difficult situations.

CRANBERRY

This small, bright-red, tart berry can be worked into
any spell or ritual focusing on love, abundance, or
protection. A worthy guest at the "thanksgiving"
table, to be sure.

GARLIC

Garlic is the magical protector and bringer of
luck, courage, health, and the inner strength
to set boundaries. Hanging a garlic braid can
deter thieves—and vampires—from entering

your home, as well as the plague. In ancient times, the pyramid builders
and Roman soldiers consumed garlic daily for its health benefits, which
extended to guarding against black magic and boosting courage. It is
nourishing, lowers blood pressure and cholesterol, and has antibiotic
properties.

    Consume before bedtime as an aphrodisiac and hang outside the
bedroom door to beckon your suitor. A garlic braid hung in children's
rooms is said to protect them from evil. Garlic given as a housewarming
gift carries heightened protective energies.

GRAPES

This simple fruit can be transformed in many ways, and help transform your intentions into reality. Grapes, when turned into wine, symbolize celebration, luxury, and abundance, and can inspire laughter, lust, truth, and affection. Wine is often incorporated into rituals where those outcomes are desired. As vinegar, a splash can protect from harm or inject a bright note to lift the mood. Eaten fresh, grapes conjure fertility, health, and success. An old Spanish tradition recognizing grapes' ability to bear luck and good fortune tells us to eat one grape for each chime of the clock at midnight on New Year's Eve—one for each month of the coming year to ensure health and happiness. Scatter them dried for long life and perseverance. Utilize the plant's leaves and vines as well as the fruit to manifest a fruitful life.

LETTUCE

Lettuce is full of healing water and the associated fluid emotions ruled by the Moon. Its green color can call money to you, or luck, or both! Lettuce harvested in fall speaks of rebirth and second chances. Use its magical charm when health or peace is threatened.

MUSHROOMS

Mushrooms have an evil reputation, not always deserved. Their long association with superstitions and witchcraft likely stems from their mysterious growth habits and seemingly spontaneous appearance in strange, oftentimes human shapes that carry malodorous stinks, as well as hallucinogenic and poisonous properties, and their quite bewitching ability to glow in the dark—not to mention kill you. They demand respect in the wild and the kitchen and should never be used, eaten, or played with if you're not 300 percent sure of what you have.

Mushrooms are creation and regeneration. They are Nature's true transformers, as they can digest and break down nearly anything. Their millions of spores are like tiny messengers sent into the world to carry on their mission and ensure the population—and their magic—never dwindles. They are communicators and relationship builders. They symbolize luck, longevity, fertility and rebirth, prosperity, safety, change, resilience, learning, intuition, patience, protection, and introspection. Their watery nature allies them with the Moon.

NUTS AND SEEDS

These culinary delights hold the keys to life. They are given to us freely as gifts from the tree spirits and flower fairies. They are tasty, nourishing, and represent good luck and abundant fertility—of ideas, relationships, and our garden's bounty. Gather them with gratitude and use them like fairy dust to spread blessings and sparkle everywhere and encourage the growth of a magical world.

ONION

Onions have a distinct dual personality. They were regarded as divine by some and born of the Devil by others. They were a food of the poor, and of the rich. They can be a supporting cast or shine as the star of the show. They are pungent and spicy, but when treated with kindness, patience, and care,  their sweetness becomes evident. They are at once whole, and yet reveal individual distinct layers. Because of these layers, Egyptians held that onions symbolized immortality—and could even bring the dead back to life! They are a reminder that life is not always as it seems, and of our role in transforming ours into the magical existence we desire. Spring onions carry all the same energies—they are simply onions pulled early in the growing season to thin the rows so those left have room to grow strong and large—and maybe give us the courage to remove from our lives what no longer serves our best selves.

PARSNIP

The lovely parsnip will sweeten your life with prosperity and your dishes with a mild, slightly nutty flavor. Left in the ground over winter, their sweetness intensifies, perhaps reminding us that instant gratification is not as rewarding as we might (sometimes) wish. Their hardy personality will boost your perseverance in working toward long-term goals.

PEAR

Sweet, juicy pears burst with the life-sustaining element of water. Their hydrating properties instantly lift the mood and impart a youthful glow, even as they offer the promise of long life and the prosperity to enjoy it. In the witch's kitchen, the pear's versatility is akin to the apple and its use with intention manifests sweet success.

POTATO

The South American Incas, not the Irish, were the first cultivators of this nutritious root vegetable, dating back thousands of years. Originally shunned by Europeans for its association with nightshades—and its ensuing belief to be poisonous—the potato did not reach Ireland until the sixteenth century, brought there by Sir Walter Raleigh, who debunked the poison theory by planting them on his property. Potato's vibrations are comforting and grounding and its magic supports perseverance, nourishment, protection, stability, and compassion. An old British tradition advises carrying raw potato in your pocket to absorb the pain of rheumatism. Blue potatoes have an otherworldly, calming vibe, and gold potatoes call in happiness and wealth. Red-skinned potatoes can ignite your passions and give you the staying power to see them to completion.

PUMPKIN (AND WINTER SQUASHES)

This fairy-tale familiar and symbol of the harvest, the pumpkin, is likely the most famous squash born of the Americas. Its use as the beloved jack-o'-lantern traces its roots to the Irish, English, and Scottish ancestors who brought the Old World tradition to North America, where the native pumpkin took over for the turnip that was originally used and a new tradition was born. Jack's original purpose was protecting hearth and home, by scaring away trickster fairies, evil spirits, and other restless souls wandering Earth, particularly on Halloween. The wide variety of pumpkins grown today is a sure indication that there's a seat at the table for everyone. It is a celebration of abundance, sustenance, and gratitude and belongs in all kitchen witch traditions.

From blossom to flesh to seeds, there are numerous, nourishing possibilities for the magical orb in the hands of a creative kitchen witch in both sweet and savory applications (save the stems, too, let them dry, and place on your altar to boost your spellwork). It also presents a perfect surface for carving sigils or initials into and, once hollowed out, a place to (safely) burn secret wishes to release their energies into the Universe. Scatter seeds to cast a circle and feed the animals and birds at the same time. Those same seeds, a symbol of fertility and abundance, left as an offering on Samhain, will nourish the wandering souls who've yet to cross over (or are just back for a visit!).

Pumpkin's magical energies will transport you to the land of your dreams where wishes come true as well as bring prosperity and attract positive vibrations. Incorporate this versatile squash into any healing dishes or spells. Its glorious shape mimics the Full Moon and channels her personality, so let pumpkin shine in any Full Moon rituals.

SWEET POTATO

Sweet potatoes, actually the root of a vine, share qualities of nourished growth while maintaining a connection with their support. They speak of loving care, home, friendship, and expansion. Their sweet taste belies their vast nutritional benefits, reminding us to look beneath the surface before making any judgments. Sweet potato's orange color ignites the sacral chakra and opens you fully to connecting with others.

TURMERIC

Golden turmeric's message is of health and healing, as well as ingenuity in making do with what's available. It offers protective and cleansing energies, which are found in its long history of ritual use for purification. Turmeric's use as an herbal medicine dates back four thousand years, and many of its health claims are bearing true under recent scientific scrutiny, including its antioxidant, antimicrobial, and anti-inflammatory properties, as well as its potential use in cancer treatment. As a spice, turmeric is widely used in South Asian and Middle Eastern cooking. Due to its color, it's been called Indian saffron. Add to homemade chicken noodle soup to boost its natural healing energies when cold or flu season hits. Add a dash of turmeric to ginger tea, and relax into its healing, warming goodness. Include the root in a healing charm bag or poppet.

SEASONAL RECIPES *and* SPELLS *for* MAGICAL LIVING

This point along the Wheel of the Year is full of gratitude and celebration for manifesting the harvest of our intentions. The foods gathered, prepared, and shared foster a communal spirit as well as a cozy atmosphere, for the kitchen hearth is kept busy with long-simmering cauldrons and hearty baked foods. It is a time for a mindful pause to reflect on growth and missteps, and a chance to share hard-earned wisdom with others. Prepare each recipe mindfully and infuse the ingredients thoughtfully. Shared purposefully, your life will be richer for it.

Love Charm Apple Butter

The cozy fall aromas alone are charming enough, but the apple butter itself is guaranteed to bring your true love to the table. With apples for love and beauty; cinnamon for abundance, power, and success and a boost to love and lust; and cloves for an aphrodisiac and the ability to boost intuition (perhaps, to recognize your intended), this recipe will work some love magic.

Makes about 2 quarts (2.2 kg)

NOTE: This is made in a 6-quart (6 L) Instant Pot, but you can also use a slow cooker. Combine as directed, cover, and cook on Low for at least 10 hours, or overnight. Blend as indicated, return to the pot on High, and cook, uncovered, until it reaches your desired consistency.

6 pounds (2.7 kg) apples (preferably organic; use a mix of types, or just your one favorite), peeled, cored, and quartered

2 tablespoons fresh lemon juice

1½ cups (340 g) packed brown sugar

½ cup (100 g) granulated sugar

1 tablespoon vanilla extract

1 heaping tablespoon ground cinnamon

½ heaping teaspoon freshly grated nutmeg

¼ teaspoon ground cloves

Generous pinch of salt

½ cup (120 ml) water

While washing the apples for this recipe, or any food, visualize any negativity or self-doubt flowing down the drain and away from you, leaving only positive vibes to infuse into your food meant to nourish others.

1. As you peel and slice the apples, put them into the Instant Pot and sprinkle with the lemon juice as you go.

2. In a medium bowl, whisk the sugars, vanilla, spices, and salt to blend. Pour the mixture over the apples, giving them a clockwise stir to call love and happiness to your life. Pour in the water, giving thanks for its easy access. Seal and lock the lid with your intentions.

3. Cook on High pressure for 90 minutes. When the cook time is up, release the pressure manually (carefully, there will be a lot of hot steam and this can take a few minutes).

4. Ladle the liquid out of the pot and into a medium bowl, reserving it. Carefully transfer the apples in small batches to a standard blender, filling it no more than half full, and blend until smooth. Alternatively, use an immersion blender right in the pot.

5. When all the apples are blended, return the apple butter to the pot and stir in some of the reserved liquid, if desired, to thin the consistency. If you like a thicker apple butter, select Sauté/Less on the Instant Pot and simmer for 15 to 30 minutes, partially covered and stirring occasionally, until the consistency is as you like it.

6. The apple butter will keep, refrigerated in an airtight container or sealed glass jar, for about 1 month. You can also freeze it (leave enough space at the top of the container for expansion) for up to 3 months. Thaw overnight in the refrigerator before use.

Just before serving, say quietly or aloud:

The apple tempts when all else fails; its heady scent a siren call.
If you, indeed, are one who's true, this apple charm will speak to you.
One taste and you are surely done, for beauty, lust, and luck have won.
So, taste my dear, the sweetness knows
two hearts alike can love as one.

Alewife's Blessings Bread

The simple act of combining a few ingredients with ground grains and turning them into life-sustaining bread, a gift both from and to the gods (and goddesses), is indeed magic. So important was wheat, many ancient cultures celebrated gods and goddesses of the wheat harvest. And the sharing, or breaking, of that bread is a universal symbol of life, peace, and hospitality. Given as a housewarming gift, bread promises that the occupants shall never know hunger. Here, the powers of wheat to manifest abundance, and beer (an ancient drink of the gods) to cleanse and bring joy, are the humble tools of the kitchen witch. Serve plain, warmed, or with honey butter or Love Charm Apple Butter (page 91) for extra blessings.

Makes one 9 × 5-inch (23 × 13 cm) loaf

Olive oil for coating the pan

3 cups (360 g) all-purpose flour

2 tablespoons fresh herbs, or 2 heaping teaspoons dried, plus more for sprinkling (I use a combination of fresh thyme, lemon thyme, oregano, and rosemary that I let dry for a few days)

1½ tablespoons plus 1 teaspoon sugar, divided

1 tablespoon baking powder

1 teaspoon kosher salt

¼ teaspoon cayenne pepper

1 packed cup (115 g) plus 2 heaping tablespoons grated sharp cheddar cheese, divided

1 bottle (12 ounces, or 360 ml) beer

While the bread bakes, invite the Greek goddess of the harvest, Demeter, to sit with you in meditation. Bread is a worthy offering for the fertile blessings she bestows.

1. Place an oven rack in the center position and preheat the oven to 375°F (190°C, or gas mark 5). Coat a 9 × 5-inch (23 × 13 cm) loaf pan with olive oil.

2. In a large bowl, stir together the flour, herbs, 1½ tablespoons of sugar, baking powder, salt, and cayenne pepper until thoroughly mixed.

3. Add 1 cup (115 g) of cheese and stir to coat in the flour mixture to keep it from sinking in the bread.

4. Pour in the beer and stir just until everything is moistened and combined into a dough ball. Spread the dough evenly in the prepared pan, infusing it with your intentions. Sprinkle with the remaining 1 teaspoon of sugar, 2 tablespoons of cheese, and a sprinkle of herbs.

5. Bake the loaf on the middle rack for about 50 minutes, or until the bread is golden brown and firm to the touch. After taking the loaf out of the oven, run a knife around the inside edges of the pan and let the bread cool in the pan for 15 minutes. Turn the loaf out onto a wire rack and let cool completely.

Before taking that first magical bite, say quietly or aloud:

*Born of the elements—air, water, earth, and fire—
crafted with magic—love, intention, abundance, and joy—
given with gratitude, may Spirit guide my soul to share my bounty
where it will do its most good.*

Hexing Harvest Nuts

These nuts, prepared two ways, can nourish a craving for salty and savory (Woodland Spice Pecans) or salty and sweet (Pumpkin Patch Pecans) as well as intentions. Whether given as gifts from your magical kitchen, shared at a party with cocktails or tea, or enjoyed mindfully for their delightful flavors and textures, these nuts can channel protection, prosperity, loyalty, luck, love, intuition, and a boost of energy to any other spells you've set in motion. Prepare to be spellbound. With gratitude to The Union Square Café for the inspiration.

Each version makes about 1 cup (140 g)

WOODLAND SPICE PECANS (SAVORY)

1 tablespoon salted butter, melted, or olive oil

1 tablespoon packed light brown sugar

1 tablespoon chopped fresh rosemary leaves, or 1 teaspoon dried (fresh is preferred for its vibrational energies and flavor)

1 teaspoon kosher salt

¼ teaspoon cayenne pepper

PUMPKIN PATCH PECANS (SWEET)

2 tablespoons salted butter, melted, or olive oil

2 tablespoons packed light brown sugar

¾ teaspoon pumpkin pie spice

¼ teaspoon ground cinnamon

Pinch of cayenne pepper

¼ teaspoon kosher salt

¼ teaspoon vanilla extract

FOR BOTH VERSIONS

1 cup (125 g) unsalted pecan halves or mixed nuts of choice

Take a moment to visualize the tree from which these nuts fell and feel the comfort of its shade, the grounding wisdom of the years it has seen, and gratitude for what it passes on to you in these gifts.

1. For either version: In a medium bowl, stir together the melted butter, brown sugar, herbs or spices, and vanilla (for the Pumpkin Patch Pecans) until well mixed.

2. In a large skillet over medium-high heat, toast the nuts for about 5 minutes, stirring frequently, until lightly browned, hot, and fragrant. Keep watch; they'll burn quickly, but you want them hot. Transfer the nuts to the bowl and stir until well coated in the spice mixture (not all of it will adhere to the nuts; let it sit for a minute or two and stir again). Store in an airtight container for 1 to 2 weeks.

Just before serving, say quietly or aloud:

I call in the grounding wisdom of truth that I may recognize my true wealth and welcome the opportunities it offers. So mote it be.

Secret Sigil Salted Caramel

This secret sauce is a sure sign of your magical powers, especially in matters of love, friendship, and connection to Spirit. Its sticky nature ensures anything you call to you while making or using this will "stick." Sugar's sweetness attracts love and happiness; water invokes transformation and the ability to adapt; butter and cream vibrate with fertility and the comfort of the Mother Goddess's embrace; salt helps protect; and vanilla boosts the love. Dip all those freshly harvested apples and pears into this caramel, or drizzle on oatmeal, ice cream, cakes for your next Cakes and Ale ceremony, or on crostini topped with cheddar and apple slices and decipher the symbols you see. Or eat right from the jar to make yourself sweetly irresistible.

Makes about 1½ cups (about 465 g)

NOTE: The magic in this recipe is that by using just your senses, a bit of patience, and staying present in the process, the alchemy happening in your kitchen cauldron will create the most luscious, cozy caramel sauce without a drop of fuss or the need for lots of equipment or even a candy thermometer.

1½ cups (300 g) granulated sugar

½ cup (120 ml) water

1 cup (235 ml) heavy cream

1½ teaspoons vanilla extract

¼ cup (½ stick, or 55 g) salted butter

1 teaspoon kosher salt

As you tend the simmering pot, reflect on needs you have simmering
just below the surface: the ones you know hold your true intentions.
Acknowledge them as they rise to the surface
and be grateful for what they teach you.

1. In a small saucepan over medium-high heat, combine the sugar and water. Cook, swirling the pan occasionally, until the sugar dissolves, the liquid starts to simmer, and the color begins to change. As the liquid cooks and begins to darken to a deeper caramel color, swirl the pan more frequently. This could take as little as 15 minutes or as long as 30 minutes, depending on your stove and the size of pan you use. Keep watch and smell: You don't want the caramel to burn—that's not the magic we're going for.

2. When the liquid has thickened, smells caramelly, and is a deep amber color, remove from the heat. Carefully whisk in the cream and vanilla—it will sputter and bubble (signs the magic's at work)— then whisk in the butter until smooth. Stir in the salt. Let cool slightly, then transfer to a glass jar with a lid and cool completely. Cover and keep refrigerated for about 1 week, if it lasts that long.

To stay mindfully in the process while the caramel transforms
on the stovetop, while waiting, say quietly or aloud:

To savor the sweetness life gives us each day,
I choose to be present in meaningful ways.
For today is a gift we have just for one day,
I promise to live it the best that I may.

Otherworldly Pumpkin Soup

The kitchen witch knows that transformation is at the heart of her magic. Here, simple ingredients transform into a warming potion to transport you away from the everyday and into that mystical place where satisfaction reigns supreme and wishes come true. Though canned pumpkin is used as a modern kitchen witch's convenience (the energies are no less meaningful), you can certainly roast and mash a peeled, cubed fresh sugar (pie) pumpkin. You'll need about 2 cups (about 425 g).

Serves 4 to 6

---

2 tablespoons olive oil

2 Honeycrisp apples, peeled, cored, and diced

1 sweet yellow onion, diced

2 cloves garlic, minced

2 to 3 teaspoons curry powder

½ teaspoon ground ginger

¼ teaspoon ground cinnamon

Freshly ground black pepper

1 can (15 ounces, or 425 g) 100% pure pumpkin

4 cups (960 ml) chicken or vegetable broth

½ cup (120 ml) heavy cream

1 tablespoon maple syrup, plus more for drizzling

Kosher salt

Roasted pepitas, for garnish

Peel an apple in one long, unbroken peel and use it to learn a bit about your intended mate. Toss the peel over your shoulder; whichever letter it forms reveals the initial of their first name! If you have a partner, use the peel to brew a lovely tea and share it to strengthen your bond. Sweeten and spice as desired.

1. In a Dutch oven over medium heat, heat the olive oil. Add the apples and onion and sauté for about 4 minutes. Stir in the garlic and sauté for 2 to 3 minutes, or until everything is softened and fragrant, taking care that the garlic does not burn. Stir in the spices, adding pepper to taste. Cook for 1 minute.

2. Stir in the pumpkin and broth. Bring the soup to a simmer. Lower the heat to maintain a simmer, cover the pot, and cook for 30 minutes, or until the apples are soft and the flavors have made friends.

3. Carefully transfer the soup in small batches to a standard blender, filling it no more than half full, and blend until smooth. Alternatively, use an immersion blender right in the pot. Return the soup to the pot and stir in the heavy cream and maple syrup. Taste and season with salt. Taste again: What secrets are revealed?

4. Serve garnished with the pepitas and a drizzle of maple syrup.

To begin your meal, and open your mind and heart to its magic, say quietly or aloud:

I bless this cauldron's healing stew, imbued with magic just for you.

The Rising Moon Cocktail

The Moon rising in the sky is always a magical sight. Dispelling darkness and inspiring awe, the Moon can help guide you if you listen with your heart.

Makes 1 enlightening cocktail

NOTE: Ice cubes made with Moon water (water infused overnight with the Full Moon's power) lend even stronger kitchen magic vibes to any potion.

Secret Sigil Salted Caramel (page 98), for drizzling

Ice

2 ounces (60 ml) vodka

1 ounce (30 ml) Kahlúa or other coffee liqueur

1 ounce (30 ml) heavy cream

*If the Moon is waxing, meditate on what's needed
to manifest your intentions; waning—assess lessons learned;
full—celebrate your achievements. Cheers!*

Drizzle the caramel sauce on the inside of an old-fashioned glass, concentrating it near the rim. Fill the glass with ice, then pour in the vodka and Kahlúa and stir to combine. Pour the cream over the top.

For an alcohol-free version: Pour the cream into a cup of freshly brewed hot or iced coffee and drizzle on a sigil with the caramel sauce.

Raise a glass to the awe-inspiring Moon, and say quietly or aloud:

May this potion set in motion a string of magic that's unbroken.

Traditional Soul Cakes

According to Irish and Scottish lore, using hazelnuts at Samhain bestows the gift of divination with sacred knowledge. They're incorporated into these cakes to appease the "soulers" as well as the ghosts and goblins, and to boost your intuition as you peer into the new year.

Makes 9 cakes

¼ cup (½ stick, or 55 g) unsalted butter, at room temperature

½ cup (115 g) packed light brown sugar

1 large egg yolk

½ teaspoon vanilla extract

1 cup (120 g) all-purpose flour, plus more for rolling

3 tablespoons very finely chopped hazelnuts

½ teaspoon ground cinnamon

¼ teaspoon ground allspice

¼ teaspoon freshly grated nutmeg

Pinch of kosher salt

2 or 3 tablespoons milk, divided

⅓ cup (50 g) raisins

Make the crosses on these cakes with intention,
each one for a loved one passed and remembered.

1. Preheat the oven to 350°F (180°C, or gas mark 4). Line a baking sheet with parchment paper.

2. In a medium bowl, use an electric handheld mixer to cream together the butter and brown sugar on medium speed until the mixture resembles wet sand (it will not be creamy). Add the egg yolk and vanilla and beat until blended.

3. Add the flour, hazelnuts, spices, salt, and 1 tablespoon of the milk. Mix until a dough begins to form. Add another tablespoon of milk and mix. Mix in the last tablespoon of milk, if needed. The dough will be soft and sticky. Stir in the raisins.

4. On a work surface, lightly flour a piece of parchment paper and a rolling pin. With lightly floured fingertips, gather the dough into a ball and place it on the prepared parchment. Roll the dough into a circle about ½ inch (1 cm) thick, dusting with more flour if it sticks to the parchment or rolling pin. Cut out 3-inch (7.5 cm) rounds with a floured cookie or biscuit cutter and transfer to the prepared baking sheet, spacing the rounds about 2 inches (5 cm) apart. The cakes will not spread much while baking.

5. Using a table knife, press the back of the blade into the top of each cake to create a cross.

6. Bake for about 20 minutes, checking after 15 minutes or so, until the soul cakes are firm to the touch and lightly golden brown. Let cool. Store in an airtight container for 2 to 3 days.

To imbue these treats with intention,
when forming the cakes say quietly or aloud:

I offer these cakes so no souls will despair,
as payment for prayers and so pranks I'll be spared.
I offer these cakes so the restless lie still,
eternally calmed by the force of my will.
I offer these cakes so their sweetness we taste,
for life's for the living, too precious to waste.

WINTER

This point on the Wheel of the Year gives us shorter days, longer nights, and much time to reflect. For the kitchen witch, it's a time to ponder ways to improve next year's harvest and reason to celebrate the extra time spent with family and friends, as Earth sleeps and renews her energies.

The harvests have been preserved to see us through this leaner time, but Earth still offers up delightfully nourishing foods to keep the magic flowing. And, though we may be deprived of daylight during this period, the kitchen and table are a place of bounty, foods imbued with the magic of memory, meaning, and tradition.

The kitchen hearth was extremely important in times past, as the warmest place in the house to gather and be protected from the cold outside. It's still the warmest place in the house, both in spirit and in temperature, and the place everyone ends up gathering. Embrace the celebration and live joyfully in the moment. The Sun will return soon enough—cherish the time of peace and joy now.

A WINTER
Blessing

Beneath the winter Moon I wait,
for warmer days, a change of fate.

Pray, goddess of the hearth and light,
do warm my soul and clear my sight;

instill in me the joy to see
the bounty you've bestowed on me.

Winter Solstice (Yule)

Winter solstice, a.k.a. Yule, falls on or about December 21 in the Northern Hemisphere (June 21 in the Southern Hemisphere) and marks the longest night of the year. It is the oldest of winter celebrations, lasting twelve days, marking the festive return of the Sun and celebrating the magic of life. It is a time of duality: of light and dark; of contemplation and anticipation; of giving and receiving; of celebration and offerings; of welcome and letting go; of death and rebirth.

Winter solstice is an anticipatory time—that time when darkness holds its breath for a moment, and we wonder whether it will ever fade. When the exhale finally comes, it's tinged with light as the Sun begins to turn its face back to us, brightening and lengthening our days and turning the calendar page on a new year. We, too, can exhale knowing, and feeling, the long winter is over. A sense of "lightness" and joy displace the dark, gloomy shadows we've kept inside these last months. To many, the Sun is a god to be worshipped and, as such, this festival has welcomed his return in many cultures around the globe for millennia.

The festival's origins are in the Scandinavian and Germanic cultures, and the festival, at one time, was connected to Norse god Odin, the father of Yule (perhaps an early precursor to Santa Claus). Others believe the Holly King, who rules over the dark part of the year, surrenders his reign to his brother, the young Oak King, who will see us through and into the lighter days of the year.

As Christianity grew throughout the world, the celebration of Christmas on December 25, which also lasts for twelve days until Epiphany, began to overlap the ancient Yule festival, and the customs and celebrations have become intertwined to some degree. Many relate Yule traditions to the Roman festival Saturnalia, honoring the Roman god Saturn, who ruled over the realm of agriculture.

It is a time of ritual, and actual, cleansing as we prepare our homes to host gatherings and celebrations, and a time of feasts, prayers, songs, and blessings in celebration of the traditions of family. Intentions are set for the calendar's new year, and we do all we can to usher in happy, lucky vibes.

Symbols of the season are many, and familiar:

- **Bells:** to ward off evil lurking in darkness

- **Candles:** to symbolize light and the return of the Sun to our days

- **Evergreens:** as the sacred Yule tree symbolizing life continuing through the dark and cold, and of healing and joy and bringing the outside in; as wreaths, symbolizing the circle of life and the Wheel of the Year

- **Holly:** for protection (the prickly leaves were thought to catch evil spirits); as a symbol of the Holly King, they bring hope

- **Ivy:** for immortality

- **Mistletoe:** to symbolize fertility and life, healing and strength

- **Sweet treats:** to delight

- **Traditional colors:** white, for light; red, for prosperity and rebirth; green, for Nature and money; gold for prosperity and wealth, giving gifts, and the Sun

- **Yule log:** traditionally ash, which has a long magical tradition, and claims a relation to the Norse Yggdrasil, or World Tree, which supports the entirety of the mythological Norse kingdom. The Yule log was traditionally lit to keep the world light while the Sun stood still, to banish evil spirits, and replace them with good luck. If it smoldered for twelve days, prosperity was guaranteed. Remnants were often kept in the house to protect it from lightning and fire; ashes were spread over the fields to ensure healthy crops.

For many a kitchen witch, winter solstice and its associated celebrations and rituals are a busy time—one filled with love and intention. Traditional foods of the season include gingerbread, wassail, foods such as ham from the traditional pig (or boar) sacrificed for the festivities, "plum" pudding and other sweets, and dried fruits, nuts, and seeds.

Gingerbread and Christmas

Gingerbread takes many forms, but "bread" is not one of them. The name derives from ginger's Latin name, *zingiber*.

In medieval times, attaining the level of master gingerbread baker within the European baking guild system was a supreme achievement and demonstration of unmatched skill and artistry. The status of these bakers was highly respected (far above the common pastry maker and bread baker) and their prosperous wages protected from competition by law: only certified gingerbread bakers were allowed to make gingerbread—except on Christmas and Easter, when anyone could make it, including citizens in their homes.

CELEBRATING YULE

Though the long, dark days have given us plenty of time to sit and reflect, it's time to turn on the lights and celebrate the return of the life-giving Sun.

- Clean your home, and especially the kitchen, with intention in preparation for guests and celebration.

- Create a Yule altar.

- Add candles to your décor and light them plentifully and safely (never leave burning candles unattended).

- Make and share recipes passed down from loved ones in an act of remembrance of the past and rebirth of the future.

- Give gifts made in your magical kitchen carrying messages of the season.

- Cut, with thanks and gratitude to Mother Nature, a Yule tree and trim it in traditional colors of the season.

- Decorate a Yule log with evergreens, pine cones, dried berries, and cinnamon sticks.

- Host a Yule feast.

- Watch the sunrise.

- Hang the mistletoe and a wreath.

- String fresh cranberries to decorate the Yule tree or hearth for protection and love.

- Stud fresh oranges, which represent the Sun, with whole cloves, for prosperity, protection, and purification, in any pattern you like—give as intention-filled gifts or use to decorate your mantel or altar.

- Spend time in meditation to contemplate the gifts of the season, or in prayer to set intentions.

- Donate to others who may not be so blessed.

Hanging the Mistletoe

The ancient Celtic Druids observed mistletoe thriving high up in the branches of the revered apple and oak trees, and held sacred its life-affirming abilities, including to stimulate fertility. With no roots to tether it to Earth, mistletoe was thought to be a manifestation of the Sun god, imbued with magical healing and protective charms.

Gathering mistletoe was a ceremony in itself, done six days after the New Moon following the winter solstice. When cut from the tree, it was caught carefully so as not to touch the ground (else its powers be gone), then distributed to townsfolk, who hung it in their doorways to ward off evil, and bestow health and good luck to all who passed beneath it. Keeping it up all year ensured a love-filled home.

In thanks to Odin for restoring their son, Baldur, to life after being killed by an arrow made of mistletoe, Norse goddess Frigg declared mistletoe a plant of love. So, hang mistletoe freely throughout your home, and especially over doorways, to protect the love nurtured there and any children at home, attract luck and good fortune, keep hale and hearty, and ward off evil spirits. But be forewarned: Refusing a kiss under the mistletoe is said to bring bad luck—so don't undo all the good you've been working to achieve with mistletoe's mysterious gifts.

Gather your mistletoe carefully and mindfully.
When ready to hang it, say quietly or aloud:

This mistletoe I hang today, keep evil spirits far away.
Everyone who shall pass beneath, I pray their health you kindly keep.
Each berry does reveal a kiss. I eagerly await the bliss.
Add luck and love and friendship dear, sweet mistletoe, do bless this year.

NOTE: Mistletoe can be poisonous to children and pets, so please do not leave it anywhere they can access it.

IMBOLC

Though the impending return of the Sun is met with much joy during
Yule, spring is still a ways off. Imbolc, also known as Candlemas (a
day when Christians brought their candles to church to be blessed)
and typically celebrated on February 2 in the Northern Hemisphere
(August 1 in the Southern Hemisphere), is another festival in honor
of the returning Sun and a day of feasting, reminding us that winter's
departure is imminent and warmer days are ahead. It is a celebration
of Earth's reawakening and a time to anticipate the next planting as we
feel Earth's fertile stirrings begin, perhaps reflected in a bit of our own
restlessness. It is a time to assess progress on intentions and do the work
needed to make them grow. The word *imbolc* means "in the mother's
belly," making it an ideal time for new beginnings.

On Imbolc, farmers worked their fields, fishers tended their boats,
and predictions were made regarding the coming weather and family
fortunes—the activities of daily life and the work of manifesting it.

In Gaelic tradition, Cailleach, goddess of weather, spent Imbolc
gathering wood for the hearth to see her through the remaining winter.
If spied on a sunny day gathering lots of wood, she was stocking up for
winter's long march. If the weather was foul and prevented her from
gathering any wood, all knew she was sound asleep and winter would
soon be over.

Another symbol of the season is milk. An alternate name for Imbolc
is Oimelc, which means "ewe's milk." This is the time when the first
lambs are born and the ewes are producing milk, both symbols of hope
and new life.

In Celtic traditions, the date also honors the Triple Goddess Brigid,
said to descend to Earth in her maiden form as the Sun, goddess of
fertility, keeper of the flame, and guardian of the hearth and home.
Tradition held that the woman of the house, while performing the

nightly chore of putting the fire to bed, pleaded with Brigid for protection of all who dwelt within. Brigid, perhaps the original kitchen witch, also represents the fires of creativity. Huge bonfires in her honor were a traditional part of the Imbolc festivities, and lit with the intention of amplifying the Sun's power.

For the kitchen witch, the flavors of Imbolc are rich, sweet, and satisfying; energies are growing and inspiring. Traditional foods honoring Imbolc are from dairy, such as butter, cheese, and milk; other foods include eggs, honey, oats, pancakes, early spring greens and herbs, the traditional Irish dish colcannon, dried fruits, seeds, and nuts, as well as anything spicy to honor the warmth of the Sun and ensure a swift return to the promise, and blessing, that is spring.

CELEBRATING IMBOLC

Signifying fresh starts and a bounty of possibilities, punctuated with the work needed to bring them to life, Imbolc celebrations are simple and rewarding:

- Light a fire in the hearth, or candles for the dining table, to imbue the home with warmth.

- Serve a cheese board with spiced wine.

- Drink eggnog sprinkled with nutmeg.

- Plan your garden (even one of intentions) and gather seeds for planting (even if only in a windowsill pot!).

- Decorate your Imbolc altar in colors of green, silver, and white.

- Fashion St. Brigid's crosses and hang them over doors and windows to protect the home.

- Journal about old and new intentions.

- Take a walk to feel the Sun on your face.

- Get up with the Sun to predict when spring will arrive!

The Magic of Winter's Bounty: Warming, Soothing, Hopeful

As winter begins, Earth has given us her many gifts to be preserved for winter nourishment, but there are some plants that prefer or continue to thrive as colder temperatures set in. These gifts can be especially sweet in actual flavor as well as intention, as food supplies can become spare during this season. Let's explore some of winter's most fabulous gifts.

AVOCADO

Believed to be native to Mexico, the avocado became part of a nutritious diet more than ten thousand years ago. In addition to nourishing the body, the Aztecs believed consuming the avocado bestowed great strength and power—both on the battlefield and in the bedroom! The word *avocado* derives from the Aztec Nahuatl word *ahuacatl*, meaning (ahem) "testicle." And although a symbol of luxury, the avocado was not always the iconic superfood it has become, teaching us that sometimes we need time to grow into our destinies. With avocado in your magical kitchen, life is fertile and full of possibilities. It will fuel your intuition to know which are ripe for the picking and creativity to make them happen. Savoring avocado's luxurious texture is a delicious act of comforting self-love. Its ability to nurture beauty inside and out is a bonus.

CAULIFLOWER

Cauliflower has definitely come into its own. Once the supporting cast for a sad vegetable tray, it is now touted as a superstar: one of the most nutritional vegetables on the planet, high in fiber, antioxidants, and anti-inflammatories, and low in calories. Magical indeed. Its (typically) white color and full, round shape channel the Moon and lend protective vibes when needed.

Cauliflower also has a bit of a trickster vibe. It can stand in for rice or steak or blend seamlessly into a sauce, so be sure your intentions are rooted in reality before calling on cauliflower to help you manifest them.

CITRUS FRUITS

Mother Nature gives us citrus just when we need it most. Coming into season in winter months, when the gloomy weather is about to take our mood under, their sunny colors and fragrance cheer us, and holding a piece of juicy citrus is like holding the Sun in your hand. When consuming citrus, visualize the sunny rays shooting from your fingertips and toes. Citrus is also full of vitamins and minerals, timed perfectly to counter the myriad winter ills battling our immune systems. Citrus is a magician's helper in the kitchen, too, lending that certain abracadabra that makes everything taste brighter and more flavorful—from sweet to savory and hot to cold, there's a use for citrus.

- **Grapefruit** delivers an instant pick-me-up and unsticks blocked energy.

- **Lemon** is always welcome for its uplifting aura and abilities to cleanse our mood as well as negative vibes in our environment, easing stress and the blues, stirring fresh, clean energy, bringing joy and clarity of purpose, and heightening confidence, intuition, and self-esteem.

- **Lime** is cheerful and fresh, cleansing, purifying, and renewing the spirit.

- **Orange** represents the Sun and encourages happiness, healing, growth, love, and friendship. It is cleansing and attracts prosperity. Oranges given as gifts create close, easy friendships.

Winter's Spice Pantry

Whether seasoning foods with a boost of flavor or intentions, a well-stocked spice pantry is a kitchen witch's ally in magic. Many of the same herbs and spices we turn to in fall (see page 82), such as nutmeg, cinnamon, ginger, and cloves, are stars in the winter kitchen. Some additional winter flavors are listed here—they are spicy, homey, and even bright, and many are thought to have protective, and lucky, properties. Add your favorites to expand the possibilities.

 Allspice: for attracting good health, good luck, and healing

Caraway seed: for true and faithful love

 **Cardamom:** for faithful love; it also calms and clears the mind

Coriander: to promote healing, health, love, and lust

 **Fennel seed:** for protection against harmful vibes, as well as an aid to cast off the old to make way for the new

Mustard seed: for protection against hexes and to strengthen your focus and intuition (black seeds); to keep evil spirits from your door, conjure love, and increase your lucky vibes (yellow seeds)

Oregano: to strengthen courage, bring happiness, foreshadow justice, stir love, boost luck, transform stress into tranquility, and help relieve the grief of losing a loved one; Aphrodite grew oregano to grow joy

Parsley: for protection against ill fates; to gain good health and honor; if in love, do not cut parsley for it will cut your connection, but when used to entice romance, it is said to promote lust and fertility

Peppermint: for clearing the mind, boosting concentration, and increasing intuitive focus

Saffron: for its universal healing energies (including hangovers!), mood-lifting capabilities, and aphrodisiac qualities (Cleopatra was said to soak in a saffron bath)

Star anise: for luck, psychic intuition, and happiness; also aids in purification

COLLARD GREENS

Collard greens, and greens in general, have a long tradition of ushering prosperity into our lives when eaten on New Year's Day. This staple of the American South grows in abundance and was a simple yet sustaining food for many. The greens' earthy flavor and dark green color are  also soothing and grounding, so don't save them for just one day a year. The long cook time required to make them soft and sweet allows plenty of space for meditating on what's needed or most important in life, and serves as an apt metaphor for accepting the changes life and age bring, softening us in many ways. Toss in some pomegranate seeds for even more abundant energy.

CRANBERRY

This jewel-toned gem of the bog is native to North America and a traditional food from Samhain through Yule. Its association with the American Thanksgiving meal is long rooted in tradition, but there is no historical evidence proving it was actually served at that first Thanksgiving celebrated by the Pilgrims.

Its festive color fits perfectly with the season and signals energy, passion, courage, rejuvenation, and rebirth. Cranberries also lend abundance, love, and healing to any kitchen spell you're crafting, so use with abandon. Being born of the bog, a place typically feared for its evil spirits and petitioned with offerings for protection, the cranberry is also protective by association.

This healthy little powerhouse is packed with vitamin C, fiber, and antioxidants, so it is a welcome addition to the plate. Its makeup is about 90 percent water, meaning a magical boost of intuition is assured when consuming this beautiful berry.

One pound (454 g) of cranberries contains about 333 cranberries. Whether divine or coincidence, the number 3 is full of luck and good fortune and represents harmony, wisdom, and understanding; past, present, and future; the Triple Goddess; and many more magically inspired ideas.

GINGER

Ginger has a long history of use as a medicinal herb and offers reassurances of safety and comfort in soothing, warming tones. Find a piece of fresh ginger that resembles a hand and picture its energies as an all-healing touch. This lovely culinary herb can be used to spice up everything from curries to gingerbread. Ginger's fiery energy increases magical powers and helps speed spells to manifestation. It is especially potent in summoning love, luck, and success. It is a warming, healing herb, noted for its immune-boosting powers.

KALE

Kale (or cale or charis) in Greek mythology was one of the Three Graces— of charm and beauty. The ancient Egyptians believed kale had the power to cure a hangover. The Irish thought it, along with its cousin the cabbage (see page 81), could foretell your future in love by pulling it up by the roots—though legend has it this worked best if the kale was stolen from someone's garden on Halloween.

As a plant, it is a prolific producer, sprouting energies of abundance, confidence, creativity (what to do with it all?!), luck, and money. Kale loves cooler temperatures and turns sweeter after a frost, signaling it's time to resolve any (frosty) disputes, let go of grudges, and move on to the goodness life has to offer. It's also one of the most nutrient-dense vegetables, supporting our health in magical ways—and we all look more beautiful when we're healthy.

KIWI

Originating in China and known as the Chinese gooseberry, the kiwifruit didn't arrive in Australia until the beginning of the twentieth century. Brought there as seeds by a missionary who gave them to a farmer who planted them where they grew into fertile trees bearing fruit seems a story of luck and divine providence. With its combination of slightly prickly and rough brown skin, guarding soft, sweet green fruit bearing abundant black seeds, a kiwi seems like it was just made for magic. This small but mighty fruit reminds us to look beneath the surface for true beauty and meaning. It also holds powers of grounding, protection, abundance and fertility, connection to Earth, money, luck, happiness, and an oversized dose of vitamin C for good health.

PERSIMMON

The persimmon's bright orange color is like the Sun returning at the winter solstice! The American persimmon's magic, aside from its sweet taste when fully ripe (*Diospyros*, the genus name, means "food of the gods"), is in

its shape-shifting abilities. Its uses are many and varied. Persimmons (locally grown) can help foretell winter weather. When you split open a seed, you'll see the image of either a fork, knife, or spoon—a fork means a mild winter; a knife predicts cutting, bitter winds; a spoon (more like a shovel!) means lots and lots of snow. American pioneers used this fruit to make persimmon beer and wine. Medicinally, its cures were wide-ranging, from diphtheria to hemorrhoids. An old folktale even suggests that simply walking by the tree could cure you of what ails! And the seeds, over time, were variously used as buttons or to make coffee, especially in the American South during the Civil War when everyday necessities were in short supply.

They're delicious in jams, puddings, pies, cookies, and muffins. The fruit was also an important food source for wildlife in winter. The wood is beautiful, similar to ebony, and any found fallen wood would make lovely magic wands, as well as magic kitchen wands, a.k.a. spoons. Because the real beauty in the persimmon is only truly appreciated when the fruit is fully ripe, it reminds us that instant gratification is not always a reward. Sometimes, waiting and working for what we really desire are the truest, sweetest rewards in life. Neither Mother Nature, nor magic, can be rushed.

RUTABAGA AND TURNIP

Rutabagas (yellow-fleshed), or Swedish turnips (named for their extreme popularity in Sweden, the reputed land of their "birth"), and turnips (white-fleshed) are often treated interchangeably, but they are two distinct vegetables, although the rutabaga has long been thought to be the result of a cabbage and a turnip getting cozy. Both belong to the Brassica family, which also includes cabbage, Brussels sprouts, broccoli, and cauliflower.

Rutabagas and turnips were both carved as jack-o'-lanterns on Halloween, before pumpkins were introduced to the custom, to scare away evil spirits and welcome the roaming spirits of those passed. Their distinct flavor can do the same to diners—some are repelled and some are drawn to them.

These sturdy root vegetables are both hardy and nourishing, and their flesh becomes sweeter once it makes it through a hard frost before harvest, reminding us that we can withstand the tough trials in life, which do, indeed, sweeten the happy times. These root vegetables are grounding and protective in their energies, and when eaten intentionally, can help heal impostor syndrome, restoring our true sense of self and worth.

Seasonal Recipes *and* Spells *for* Magical Living

The element of fire is evident in your kitchen magic right now. Long-simmering foods that warm and soothe dominate this time of the Wheel, and in batches big enough to be shared to create bonds and memories. Hearty spices ensure life's never dull and sweet treats lighten the mood. A glass of good cheer toasts warm days to come and colorful foods deliver wishes for great joy—as well as nutrition to keep us healthy and happy. Traditions dominate, connecting us to times past and loved ones passed. Honor the old but celebrate the new as you cook up a magical season for all.

Hot Buttered Rum

Rum celebrates love and can enhance spirituality. Brown sugar ensures sweet outcomes, and spices offer abundant, creative, and protective energies. Butter eases change and makes a great goddess gift. A sip of this on a cold winter's day will channel the warmth of the emerging Sun and awaken your dreams. Double the batch for a group celebration, such as when welcoming the coven to your home.

Batter makes enough for 5 warming drinks; recipe makes 1 drink

---

FOR THE HOT BUTTERED RUM BATTER

¼ cup (½ stick, or 55 g) unsalted butter, at room temperature

¼ cup (60 g) packed dark brown sugar

1 teaspoon vanilla extract

½ teaspoon ground cinnamon

½ teaspoon freshly grated nutmeg

¼ teaspoon ground cloves

Pinch of kosher salt

FOR THE HOT BUTTERED RUM

1½ ounces (45 ml) dark rum

6 ounces (180 ml) very hot (not boiling) water

While waiting for the water to heat, contemplate who may need a bit of extra love shown to them at this time.

1. To make the batter: In a medium bowl, combine all the batter ingredients. Using an electric handheld mixer, or a sturdy spoon, mix on medium speed until well blended and creamy.

2. To make the hot buttered rum: Place 1 tablespoon of batter into a mug and pour in the rum. Stir in 4 ounces (120 ml) of the hot water until the batter dissolves. Stir in the remaining 2 ounces (60 ml) of water.

3. The remaining batter will keep refrigerated in an airtight container for up to 6 months (but why wait that long to celebrate?).

FOR AN ALCOHOL-FREE VERSION: Omit the rum and water and stir 1 cup (240 ml) of hot apple cider or apple-spiced tea into the batter.

When ready to toast to good cheer, say quietly or aloud:

With one sweet sip this warming brew does melt my fears away.
And in their place I wish for dreams that conjure happy days.

Pomegranate Jewels Salad

An average pomegranate contains up to six hundred deliciously juicy seeds. Imagine the lift to your intentions if you imbue them into this delectable fruit before eating!

Serves 4

½ cup (50 g) pecan halves

1 teaspoon Boar's Head Festival Mustard Caviar
(page 134) or Dijon mustard

Pinch of kosher salt

Freshly ground black pepper

¼ teaspoon dried thyme leaves

1 tablespoon maple syrup or honey

3 tablespoons apple cider vinegar

5 tablespoons extra-virgin olive oil

1 large head curly endive or green leaf lettuce,
trimmed and coarsely chopped

1 Honeycrisp apple or other sweet apple, cored, halved,
and thinly sliced into half-moons

½ cup (90 g) pomegranate seeds

Shaved Parmesan cheese, for garnish (optional)

*Before tossing the pomegranate seeds into the salad, make a wish, eat
three seeds, and prepare for your wish to come true.*

1. In a small skillet over medium-high heat, toast the pecans, stirring
   frequently, for about 5 minutes, or until lightly browned and
   fragrant. When cool enough to handle, roughly chop the nuts.

2. In a small jar with a tight-fitting lid, combine the mustard, salt, a
   few grinds of pepper, thyme, maple syrup, vinegar, and oil. Seal
   the lid and shake well until blended and emulsified.

3. In a large bowl, combine the greens, apple, pomegranate seeds,
   and toasted pecans. Pour half the dressing over the salad, giving
   thanks for the fresh foods on your table, and toss to coat and
   combine. Garnish with Parmesan, as desired, and serve with the
   remaining dressing on the side. Let the beauty of this salad be an
   offering to all at your table.

When ready to make your wish, say quietly or aloud:

*These seeds I hold bring wishes bold, with wealth enough to share.
Sweet ruby jewels, my magic tools, grant riches beyond compare.*

GRATITUDE GRANOLA

This gracious granola makes a great gift from any kitchen witch. Add each ingredient to the batch with intention and give each gift with the accompanying "recipe" (or spell), with gratitude for friendship and to share a bit of magical living.

Makes about 10 cups (1.2 kg)

½ cup (120 ml) vegetable or olive oil, plus more for the pan

4 cups (360 g) old-fashioned oats

1 cup (85 g) unsweetened coconut flakes

1 cup (95 g) unsalted sliced almonds

1 cup (100 g) unsalted pecan halves

½ cup (70 g) salted sunflower kernels or (65 g) pepitas

6 tablespoons packed dark brown sugar

2 tablespoons ground cinnamon

½ cup (120 ml) maple syrup

2 teaspoons vanilla extract

½ teaspoon kosher salt

½ cup (70 g) diced pitted Medjool dates

1 cup (145 g) golden raisins

In the traditions of the kitchen witch, the magical oven stands in for the Sun, or the bonfires of Yule and Imbolc, transforming the individual ingredients into a singular message: gratitude.

1. Preheat the oven to 350°F (180°C, or gas mark 4). Lightly coat a large rimmed sheet pan with oil.

2. To begin the spell, in a large bowl, stir together the oats, coconut flakes, nuts, seeds, brown sugar, and cinnamon until well distributed and imbued with your intentions.

3. In a medium bowl, whisk the oil, maple syrup, vanilla, and salt until well combined. Stir the liquid ingredients into the oat mixture until all is well coated and protected. Spread the granola in an even layer on the prepared sheet pan.

4. Bake for 15 minutes; stir. Bake for about 15 minutes more, or until the granola starts to look toasted, keeping an eye on it so it does not burn. Let cool for 15 minutes. Take the time to absorb the fragrance and let it fill you with joy.

5. Stir in the dates and raisins. Let cool. Store in an airtight container at room temperature for up to 2 weeks.

When ready to assemble and nourish the spirit, say quietly or aloud:

*Oats create the foundation that supports happiness
and nourishes family and abundance.
Dates and raisins honor the life-giving Sun and breed fertility.
Almonds bring luck and love; coconut, for new beginnings.
Vanilla opens the heart.
Cinnamon grants abundance, love, power, and success.
Pecans bestow wealth; sunflower seeds ensure wishes are granted.
Maple syrup grounds us, supporting health and longevity.
Oil guards against evil and salt protects.
Brown sugar's sweetness boosts the energy of this spell that all who
enjoy it know a flavorful life.*

Holly and Ivy Gingerbread with Sunny Lemon Sauce

The sticky nature of molasses is perfect for bringing together and binding two things; its slow-moving habit tells us not to hurry—magical things will happen in their own good time. Celebrate the flavors of the season with this rich gingerbread, and give a nod to the emerging Sun with the bright lemon sauce ladled over the top. If you prefer, serve with a dollop of whipped cream in honor of Imbolc.

Serves 9, plus about 1¼ cups (300 ml) sauce

FOR THE GINGERBREAD

¼ cup (½ stick, or 55 g) unsalted butter, at room temperature, plus more for the pan

2 cups (240 g) all-purpose flour

1½ teaspoons baking powder

½ teaspoon baking soda

½ teaspoon kosher salt

2 teaspoons ground ginger

1 teaspoon ground cinnamon

¼ teaspoon ground allspice

½ cup (115 g) packed dark brown sugar

½ cup (120 ml) molasses

1 large egg

1 cup (240 ml) buttermilk

FOR THE LEMON SAUCE (OPTIONAL)

1 cup (240 ml) water

½ cup (100 g) granulated sugar

2 tablespoons cornstarch

⅛ teaspoon freshly grated nutmeg

Pinch of salt

2 tablespoons unsalted butter

¼ cup (60 ml) fresh lemon juice

1 teaspoon grated lemon zest

As you make this cake, reflect on whatever darkness in life is bothering you and what you would like to replace it with. As you make the lemon sauce, inhale the uplifting aroma and let it dissolve the darkness.

1. Preheat the oven to 350°F (180°C, or gas mark 4). Generously coat an 8-inch (20 cm) square baking dish with butter.

2. To make the gingerbread: In a medium bowl, whisk the flour, baking powder, baking soda, salt, and spices to blend. Mixing counterclockwise will help banish anything unwanted from your orbit. Set aside.

3. In a large bowl, using an electric handheld mixer, cream together the ¼ cup (55 g) of butter and brown sugar on medium speed until well blended. Add the molasses in three additions, blending well after each addition until the butter mix is smooth. Add the egg and blend until well mixed.

4. Alternating the dry ingredients and the buttermilk, add to the butter mixture in three additions, ending with the buttermilk, and mixing well after each addition until the batter is fully blended and no flour streaks remain. Scrape the batter into the prepared pan and smooth the top.

5. Bake for 35 minutes, or until a toothpick inserted into the center comes out clean. Let cool.

6. To make the lemon sauce (if using): While the cake bakes, in a small saucepan over medium-high heat, whisk the water, granulated sugar, cornstarch, nutmeg, and salt. Cook, whisking frequently, until the sauce starts to boil. Remove from the heat and whisk in the 2 tablespoons of butter, lemon juice, and lemon zest until the butter melts. Let cool.

7. The gingerbread will keep, covered at room temperature, for 3 to 4 days. Refrigerate the sauce in an airtight container for up to 5 days. Let the sauce come to room temperature before using.

Drizzle the sauce over the cake in any shape, or sigil, symbolic of your intention. While drizzling, say quietly or aloud:

Of Sun and light and smiles bright, enchant us with your tales.
Of sweet and tart, do fill my heart with hope that never fails.
Of heat and spice, let love entice the wind to fill our sails.

Witch's Wassail

Wassail, from the Old English word *was hál*, means to be of hale, or good, health. The original tradition of wassailing revelers out and about to ensure the good health of the coming year's apple harvest is brought inside here: a toast from the bowl is full of abundant cheer and wishes for everyone's good health and success, plus the magical energies of cinnamon and clove's prosperity and protection. Scale the good cheer up or down depending on the size of your gathering and let the songs begin.

Makes about 6 cups (1.4 L)

---

2 oranges

Whole cloves

4 cups (960 ml) apple cider or apple juice

2 cups (475 ml) cranberry juice

9 cinnamon sticks

6 ounces (180 ml) bourbon or rum (optional)

As you insert the cloves into the orange, visualize each as a step closer to the success you desire.

1. Stud one orange all over with cloves in any pattern you like. Thinly slice this orange, then cut the slices into half-moons.

2. In a saucepan over medium-low heat, combine the apple cider, cranberry juice, and the juice of the remaining orange—breathe in the uplifting aromas; let them fill you with warmth and ease. Add 3 of the cinnamon sticks and let the wassail warm for about 15 minutes. Keep an eye on it; you don't want it to boil. Transfer the wassail to a heatproof punch bowl, or a slow cooker to keep

warm, and stir in the bourbon (if using; or let everyone add their own—or not—to their wassail cup). Float the orange half-moons in the wassail and serve each cup with a cinnamon stick for fragrant stirring, clockwise, of course.

With filled glass in hand, say quietly or aloud:

A drink to one's health, a toast to next year;
I see wealth in all forms reaped with wassail's good cheer.

Boar's Head Festival Mustard Caviar

Mustard originally grew as a weed, until it was cultivated for its own sake in classical Greek times. Since then, mustard seed has been made into and used as a condiment for thousands of years, and has even been served as a medicine. In the traditional English Yule log festival, the presentation of the boar's head was accompanied by mustard for serving. Try this delightful condiment anywhere you'd normally use mustard, especially on pork, hamburgers, or sandwiches, blend into vinaigrettes, or stir into sauces to brighten the flavors. Brown mustard seeds invite protection and strengthen intuition, whereas yellow mustard seeds keep evil from your door and increase lucky vibes.

Makes about ½ cup (135 g)

2 tablespoons brown mustard seeds

2 tablespoons yellow mustard seeds

6 tablespoons apple cider vinegar

3 tablespoons water

2 tablespoons sugar

1½ teaspoons honey

1 bay leaf

Pinch of kosher salt

Few grinds of black pepper

Set your intentions for this mustard caviar with care. The tiny mustard seeds burst with a bit of joy, and are a tangible reminder of the intentions you're working to manifest every time you bite into them.

In a small skillet over medium-high heat, combine all the ingredients. Bring the mixture to a boil. Decrease the heat to maintain a low simmer and cook for about 45 minutes, or until the liquid is mostly reduced and the seeds are tender but still pop. If the caviar looks dry, add 1 tablespoon of water at a time to keep from burning. Remove and discard the bay leaf. Let cool, transfer to a jar with a tight-fitting lid, and keep refrigerated for 2 to 3 weeks.

When ready to serve, take a moment to visualize your intentions coming to fruition, then say quietly or aloud:

With each seed is the chance to heed that which my heart desires.

SPRING

As the Wheel of the Year begins to turn its face to the Sun, this new season of hope and renewal is full of magical living. For the kitchen witch, there's a simple joy to trying new foods, recipes, or potions and, perhaps, a reawakening of spirit that comes with a renewed closeness with Earth, especially if tending a kitchen garden. The air, soil, water, and sunshine seem to burst with energy and beckon you to them.

The warming Sun eases Earth back into motion, and the foods that will grace our table in months to come begin as the seeds of intention planted in Earth as she seduces you near.

There is an unmistakable feeling of joy, optimism, and energy vibrating as the world begins to shake off its winter coat and bursts into its springtime best. Possibilities are endless and life is a celebration.

Foods are fresh, clean, light, and hydrating, as if they know just what our bodies need after a long winter's nap. Green dominates, but then so does creativity and the ability to see newness in every glance. Fertility and abundance are at work, and manifestation is yours for the asking. What does your heart desire?

A SPRING
Blessing

May the change that is spring renew hope in our hearts; may the change be a joyful rebirth.

May the warmth of the Sun ease the darkness within; may my light be the beacon for others.

With great thanks for new life that emerges from Earth, may it feed bodies as well as our spirits.

May the awe of it all as the beauty unfolds reveal life's magic and glorious gifts.

OSTARA

As Earth wakes from her winter's rest, an aura of green, with its sweet scent, begins to shimmer to life. At this time of heightened fertility on Earth, Ostara celebrates the spring equinox, generally March 21 in the Northern Hemisphere (September 21 in the Southern Hemisphere), and its energies of rebirth, renewal, and new possibilities. Ostara (or Eostre), the Teutonic goddess, was goddess of springtime and mother of the dawn, who brings with her warming winds and the joy of newness. It is a time to plant seeds in the garden and nurture those seeds of intention germinating since Imbolc. It is a time to celebrate fresh starts and the winds of change, and to seek balance in life as light and dark in our days become equal.

Ostara was originally celebrated on Easter, which occurs nearby, on the Sunday following the first Full Moon after this March equinox, marking it on a different date each year, and so you can find influences of Ostara in its celebration today.

Symbols of Ostara include the egg and hare, both with recognizable histories as symbols of fertility and life, as well as fairies, fresh flowers, and butterflies. How all the symbols and the festivities and the goddess become so intertwined and, eventually, birthed the legend of the Easter Bunny is a topic of much debate, but one simple version goes like this: The goddess Ostara came upon an injured bird who could no longer fly. To heal the bird and ensure it survived the winter, she turned it into a hare. To thank Ostara, every year on her celebration day, the hare, in bird-like fashion, lays beautifully colored eggs in her honor. Bonfires and feasts were also part of the traditional celebrations.

For the kitchen witch, flavors are simple and fresh; energies are vibrating with change and expectation. Traditional foods include baked goods, eggs, honey, asparagus, peas, lettuce, and sprouts. Baskets are also symbolic of this celebration.

Connecting *with* Plant Energy

In addition to the energy of the elements—fire, air, water, and earth—you have the power of plant energy to harness for your kitchen magic. Plant energy combines the four basic elements plus the individual nature of the plant itself, including its color correspondence. This is particularly energizing in spring, when vibrations are running high everywhere, but is something you may want to do each season, to really attune to Nature's rhythms.

When your kitchen garden, a local park, the potted plant by your doorstep, or a favorite tree begins to bloom and grow, step among Nature and use all five senses (taste, wisely, if something is available) to tune in to the plants' energy.

- What do you see? Are you drawn to any particular plant by its smile?

- Gently touch that plant, or any other: What do you feel? How does it make you feel?

- Softly brush the plant or turn your face to the breeze. What do you smell?

- Listen. Can you hear the plants' soft hellos? What messages pop into your mind?

- Are there fresh berries, herbs, fruits, or vegetables you can sample (with permission)? What do you taste? (If not, that's okay; there will be another time.) What does that taste conjure in you?

Take a few moments to just "be" with the plants. Let their energy inspire you. You may be surprised by what you learn from them.

CELEBRATING OSTARA

Signifying change and a restoring of balance, try the following to celebrate Ostara:

- ❀ Refresh your altar with daffodils and something green.

- ❀ Do some spring cleaning.

- ❀ Make quiche filled with asparagus or sprinkled with chives.

- ❀ Dye some eggs, then organize an egg hunt.

- ❀ Cook over an open fire.

- ❀ Rise at dawn to welcome the new day.

- ❀ Plant some seeds in your kitchen garden or in a pot.

- ❀ Take a walk and identify as many returning birds as you can.

- ❀ Feed the returning birds.

- ❀ Eat some chocolate!

BELTANE

Occurring on May 1 in the Northern Hemisphere (November 1 in the Southern), also known as May Day, this ancient pagan Celtic festival of flowers, fires, fertility, and sensuality celebrates the coming of summer and Earth's nascent fertility. This time on the Wheel of the Year is a time of planting and an acknowledgment of the cycle of birth, growth, and death that defines life.

Beltane, which means "the fires of Bel" (referring to the Celtic Sun god, Belenus, thought to be the Celtic equivalent of Apollo, and often associated with the Celtic god Lugh, see page 172), signals the strong presence of the Sun and its influence on lush crop growth. And like Samhain, this is a time, especially on the Eve of Beltane, also known as Walpurgis Night, when the veils between worlds is thin, and witches and fairies are most active. Revelers beware!

Huge bonfires were lit as symbols of celebration (and to protect against the spellbinding witches and fairies) and were festive gathering places for the locals, where much dancing and merrymaking ensued. The fires, too, symbolized cleansing and a chance for the community to renew itself as they emerged from the dark winter months. Even the cattle were released from their barns and put out to live and grow in the pasture, being driven there between the bonfires to symbolically cleanse them of disease and ensure their fertility.

In ancient times, the homes' hearth fires would have been extinguished before the festival and relit with the flames of the bonfires.

Dairy, oats, breads, fiery foods, and honey are traditional foods for Beltane feasts. And, as it is a time when the Sun god joins the Earth goddess in a wedding of sorts, any celebratory foods found at weddings are welcome.

CELEBRATING BELTANE

Celebrating fertility, beauty, and love, in all its manifestations in life, to mark Beltane:

- Dance like no one is watching.

- Roast marshmallows over an open fire.

- Drink milk, as an offering to the mischievous fairies known to sour it on Beltane; you might offer them a sip, too.

- Pick a bouquet of fresh flowers and weave them into a wreath to wear on your head.

- Decorate a Maypole, or make mini Maypoles as magical wands.

- Wash your face and hair in the morning dew (especially gathered from lady's mantle), ensuring goddess-like beauty and a glowing complexion.

- Indulge in a spa treatment or ritual beauty bath.

- Fill May baskets with foods and gifts for those in need.

- Host a Beltane feast.

- Propose a toast to the happy couple, Sun and Earth, with May Wine (page 156).

- Plant sweet woodruff in your kitchen garden for that pitcher of May Wine.

- Light a candle.

- Leave an offering of clean water for the fairies' refreshment.

- Cast a love spell.

- Perform a fertility ritual.

The Magic of Spring's Bounty: Fresh and Awakened

Is it any coincidence that many of spring's most beloved foods bring energies of abundance and fertility? This is the time of fresh starts, new ideas, unbridled optimism and excitement, and dreams of "What's next?" You'll find all that and more in spring's harvest, along with some options to keep you grounded in reality (while continuing to dream), protect your energy and successes, and bolster courage and perseverance to see things through to the end. There is no lack of flavor here, so savor all life gives you and feed your magic accordingly.

ARTICHOKE

This member of the thistle family is native to the
Mediterranean region. Greek mythology tells us
we owe the artichoke's origins to the duplicitous
Zeus falling in love at first sight with the maiden
bathing beauty Cynara, whom he promptly seduced,
promoted to goddess, and installed in his pantheon on Mount Olympus.
But this simple girl missed her family and so snuck off the mountain to
visit them. On discovery, this so enraged Zeus that he hurled her off
the mountain and turned her into an artichoke, which has been gracing
tables ever since, both as a delicacy and as an aphrodisiac.

As you prepare artichokes, relish the process of removing each
protective layer to reach the true and perfect heart and imagine the
joy you'll feel on fully opening your heart, without defenses, to life
around you. Those prickly petals can be perfect for defensive magic as
well, when protection from harm is needed. Considering its origins, the
artichoke can also heal a broken heart, restore balance after a storm of
emotions, expose the truth, and promote love. Savor each delicious leaf.

ARUGULA

Though the ancient Romans enjoyed arugula, also
known as rocket, on their tables, it took a while for
its popularity to gain a foothold elsewhere in the
world. All this is said to remind us that good things
happen to those who wait and magic can't be hurried.
Its earliest fans favored the green for its ability to stir the heart and
loins (though methinks almost any food can be assigned this ability if
you like it enough . . .) and its peppery flavor can certainly spice up a
salad. Arugula can also give a boost to your intuition and help repel any
negative influences you may detect.

ASPARAGUS

From ancients to royals and everyone in between, asparagus is much loved in the kitchen. This "magic wand" of the vegetable kingdom is full of spells—as well as vitamins, fiber, and minerals—and just waiting for you to pick it up. It is one of the first spring vegetables to stretch its face to the Sun, confirming spring, indeed, has sprung, signaling rebirth and all the hope that comes with it. Its suggestive shape puts it squarely in the aphrodisiac category and its seeming ability to grow right before your eyes speaks of abundance and fertility. Eating asparagus instills us with the patience to work toward our goals: The first harvest does not happen until the plant is four years old, and only then for a brief period, letting the roots develop more fully. This also reminds us of the importance of self-care, and tending to our roots to keep them strong, whether that's family, religious beliefs or traditions, or whatever supports us in our day-to-day lives. Your rewards will multiply quickly!

Coming in shades of green (wealth), purple (authority, intuition), pink (compassion, joy), and white (peace, protection), asparagus is associated with cleansing and can be infused with your intentions for such, as needed.

CELERY

Historically, celery is touted for its alluring aphrodisiac qualities—perhaps its provocative shape is to blame. Its watery nature and preference for cooler climates are naturally calming and restful and help cleanse the mind of worrisome thoughts to stay focused on priorities and maintain a cheerful outlook. Its flavor and texture make it a standard go-to as a base layer for soups, salads, casseroles, and more. The ancient Romans believed celery cured headaches—especially the nasty hangover type, as it cured the hangover, too. Bloody Mary, anyone?

Spring's Spice Pantry

Whether seasoning foods with a boost of flavor or intentions, a well-stocked spice pantry is a kitchen witch's ally in magic. For seasonal spring flavors, dried spices may begin to take a lesser role in your kitchen magic as fresh herbs appear in the garden. When the spice pantry is used in spring, the flavors are brighter, letting the taste of the fresh foods shine with energies of health, joy, love, luck, and protection. And, of course, don't forget fresh citrus as part of your spice pantry. It's especially good at this time of year to add a splash of sunny flavor. Add your favorites to expand the possibilities.

Basil: to breed courage, forgiveness, good wishes, love, and wealth

Cilantro: for health and healing, love and lust, money magic and abundance

Coriander: to promote healing, health, and love

Garlic: to give courage, health, inner strength, love, luck, and protection

Mint: to magnify the power of our words, refresh our spirits, and protect travelers

Oregano: to strengthen courage, bring happiness, foreshadow justice, stir love, boost luck, transform stress into tranquility, and help relieve the grief of losing a loved one; Aphrodite grew oregano to grow joy

Parsley: for protection against ill fates; to gain good health and honor; if in love, do not cut parsley for it will cut your connection, but when used to entice romance, it is said to promote lust and fertility

Rosemary: for fidelity, mental clarity, remembrance, and protection from thieves

Tarragon: to inspire courage and confidence

Thyme: to imbue courage, activity, health, and healing; attract affection and loyalty; and remove negative energy

CHIVES

Chives speak of usefulness and practicality, and this spring delight can add a bit of magic to just about any savory dish—and the lovely purple blossoms are also edible and dry beautifully. In the early history of chives' use, they eased melancholy and banished evil spirits. Chives season life with joy and courage as well as guard against illness and harmful spirits when hung in the doorway—they'll even deter pests when planted in your garden. They're effective at helping break bad habits, especially concerning weight loss. Chives are easy to grow, even in a pot, so they can be part of every kitchen witch's garden.

CILANTRO

This generous plant is two in one—in the United States, the fresh leaves are known as cilantro and the seeds (berries), when dried, are the slightly sweeter coriander. Its language of flowers speaks to hidden worth. The herb is said to be an aphrodisiac and it is thought that the Chinese used it in love potions, believing it also bestowed immortality. It was so sacred in Egypt that it was buried with the pharaohs. This ancient herb—thought to have been grown in the Hanging Gardens of Babylon—has long been used to promote healing, health, love, and lust. Its green color makes cilantro appropriate for money magic, too. If grown in your home or kitchen garden, it brings about peace and cooperation, which may be apt, as this fresh herb is either loved or reviled!

EGG

This symbol of fertility and the circle of life comes naturally packaged in a perfectly protective shell and reminds us of the importance of nurturing life in all its forms as well as setting boundaries to keep away what harms. Perhaps the most mythical of all foods, eggs symbolize spring and rebirth, freshness and opportunity. Variously, eggs have hatched gods, Earth, the heavens, the Sun, and the entire Universe all at once. Imagine, even, the mystery of a tiny bird hatching from an egg.

Eggs have been used to accompany the dead into the afterlife, divine the future, diagnose illness, banish the evil eye, and boost fertility (in people and Earth). After eating a cooked egg, the shell should be crushed to avoid bad luck—or the random witch from using it as a boat in which to travel the world wreaking havoc wherever she goes.

Decorating eggshells, a tradition that goes back some sixty thousand years, remains a popular practice today, often to celebrate new life and resurrection.

The egg is an almost perfect food, offering a combination of proteins, fats, vitamins, and minerals that sustain life. For the kitchen witch, the egg is a symbol of not only Ostara but also pure magic. It can be eaten on its own or made into hundreds of other dishes, both sweet and savory. Before cooking them, imbue the raw eggs with your intentions. As a symbolic womb, the egg will incubate your messages and, once broken, release them into the Universe to be heard and acted upon.

FIDDLEHEADS

Long an early spring tradition, gathering fiddleheads (the young, unfurled, edible tips of the ostrich fern), some of the first greens to emerge from winter's grip, with a quiet request for approval from Mother Nature, is a joyful celebration of new life emerging from Earth. The time to gather them, before they open, is fleeting, reminding us that life is as well and we should live each moment fully and mindfully.

NOTE: The ostrich fern grows in parts of Canada and the United States, Central Europe, Scandinavia, Russia, Asia, Great Britain, and Ireland. However, *most fern species are poisonous*, so unless you're well versed in identification, consider adding them to your kitchen garden, or foraging from your local grocer or farmers' market instead of the woods or wild.

Ferns are at once prehistoric (having been around longer than dinosaurs) and enchanting. Because of their (then) mysterious propagation—the fern produces neither flower nor seed—it was deduced that the seeds of a fern must be invisible. Legend tells us that anyone carrying fern seeds in their pocket will also be invisible! And (logically?) that invisible seed must be born of the invisible flower, which is said to bloom but once a year at midnight on the summer solstice. Should you be lucky enough to spy said flower, you will be happy and rich for eternity.

Ferns have been used to heal, promote longevity, symbolize rebirth and new beginnings, and increase one's luck in love. They also represent humility. Burning ferns or pulling them up by the roots (ouch!) will also bring on cleansing storms. The lovely fern can also boost the energy of other magical herbs, protect from evil witches, and improve mental clarity.

KOHLRABI

Like its cousin the cabbage, kohlrabi is protective, both in its mystical energies and in its nutritional benefits. The alien appearance of this vegetable may hint at its ability to enhance otherworldly connections. It is a versatile vegetable in the magic kitchen, offering up both stems and roots to be eaten, either raw or cooked.

PEAS

Peas have such sweet magical energy . . . all nestled like babes in their protective cocoon of a shell, they evoke family, friendship, growth, and protection—or of lucky coins tucked into a purse and the vibrations to pull money and success your way. Their vining growth habit gives them tenaciousness and confidence to reach beyond their comfort zone, while their roots keep them firmly grounded.

Peas have been around so long that even their origins seem magical, certainly mystical. And for every recalcitrant, pea-hating child, they might relate to the tale that the Norse believed peas were a punishment sent by Thor to rebellious worshippers.

PINEAPPLE

A longstanding symbol of wealth and welcome, the pineapple's sunny hue is sure to bring a smile. Once a scarce luxury afforded by few—hence its early use as purely decorative rather than to eat—pineapples can now be enjoyed at will. Pineapples exude strength and power. They bring wealth, good fortune, and good luck and can increase confidence and personal magical energy as well as strengthen psychic information flow and intuition. Among the pineapple's most magical attributes are youthfulness, immortality, and regeneration.

RADISH

The radish originated in China thousands of years ago, where it has a long use in traditional Chinese medicine to help balance energy and improve digestion, and was one of the first vegetables introduced in the New World. The Greeks offered golden replicas to Apollo, signifying their importance, and Egyptian pharaohs enjoyed the vegetable long before the pyramids were constructed. Planted in spring under the New Moon, it's said, will produce the best harvest. Both the familiar root of the plant and the leaves are edible. Their innate heat and quick growth cycle boost manifesting energies of any spellwork. An old Germanic superstition tells that wearing a crown of wild blue radish flowers gives one the ability to detect witches.

SPINACH

For the kitchen witch looking for magical ingredients, spinach reaches superfood status and can do the kind of magic in our bodies that keeps us strong and healthy. Its green color speaks of abundance and money magic, and as one of the first vegetables ever frozen for commercial use (thank you, Mr. Birdseye), it brings strength to take risks and reap the rewards. And though spinach leaves are quite delicate looking and easy to cook, this plant can survive, even thrive, over cold winters, teaching us we're tougher than we look and that rough times can only make us stronger and more forgiving.

STRAWBERRY

In the language of flowers, the sweet strawberry speaks of perfection, intoxication, and delight. It is said to be a favorite fruit of the goddess Frigg (see page 33), for whom guarding marriages was a duty, and  served as an apt symbol of Venus, goddess of love, because of its heart shape and red color. Its abundance of seeds—borne proudly and uniquely on its exterior—has long represented sexuality. Its tenacious vining habit and ability to grow in even adverse conditions teach us that perseverance is key to success.

An old Bavarian custom, still honored today, says that baskets of strawberries tied to cattle's horns will please the elves, and they, in return, will bless the cattle to ensure health and an abundant milk production. Perhaps the origins of strawberries and cream?!

The strawberry's three-part leaves are interpreted as the Holy Trinity, making it a preferred adornment of churches and crowns during the Middle Ages. In Tudor England, Anne Boleyn was said to have been marked as a witch by the strawberry birthmark she bore on her neck, causing widespread avoidance of the fruit by pregnant women all over England. The English nobility distinguishes some of its rank, namely Duke, Marquess, and Earl, in their coronets by the number of strawberry leaves and the type of material (gold or silver) from which they're made, perhaps as a reminder of their humble origins.

Where there are strawberries, there is love, creativity, fertility, and success.

SWEET WOODRUFF

Also known as "kiss me quick," this delightful herb lives up to its sweet name. This fast-growing herb is a beauty in the garden, where its delicate white flowers light up shady spaces. It was widely used as a room freshener in times past, whether strewn on the floor, hung in a room, mixed into a potpourri, or used to stuff a lady's mattress with its sweet scent.

Medieval soldiers believed sweet woodruff brought them protection in battle, which may have been due to its mildly anesthetic properties and ability to induce joy. It is also known to have antioxidant and anticoagulant properties. Wreaths of sweet woodruff frequently adorned churches, as a symbol of humility.

A traditional component of May Wine (page 156), the flowers and leaves are edible, and make a lovely tea, or a delightful enchantment to fruit salad.

Call on sweet woodruff for money issues, especially when abundance is desired, as well as strength to face any battle looming, or to invite that quick kiss you may desire (along with love)!

SEASONAL RECIPES *and* SPELLS *for* MAGICAL LIVING

This season on the Wheel of the Year infuses newness into your kitchen magic. Although tried and true gets the results you're after, shaking things up a bit with new cuisines, new foods, or new recipes may be just the energy you need to manifest intentions. Whatever you cook up, it's easy to get the best results using the freshest ingredients, and that is what this season is all about.

WITCHING HOUR COCKTAIL

This lovely libation is just the thing to encourage a little introspection.
The influence of violet here promotes honest communication, in this
case with yourself, and its springtime scent can soothe and uplift.

Makes 1 bewitching cocktail

Ice

1½ ounces (45 ml) citrus vodka

1 ounce (30 ml) crème de violette

1 ounce (30 ml) sour mix (preferably homemade)

3 ounces (90 ml) Champagne or other sparkling white wine

Lemon peel, for garnish (optional)

*When shaking this cocktail, do so with purpose to harmonize your
intentions and ready them to be released to work their magic.*

In a cocktail shaker filled with ice, combine the vodka, crème de
violette, and sour mix. Cover and shake for about 30 seconds
to chill. Pour in the Champagne, stir lightly, and strain into a
Champagne flute. Squeeze the lemon peel over the drink and drop
it into the cocktail (if using). So mote it be!

FOR AN ALCOHOL-FREE VERSION: Combine 1 ounce (30 ml) violet
simple syrup with 6 ounces (180 ml) lemon-lime soda. Add ice, and
adjust the syrup to taste.

When ready to receive the messages meant for you, say quietly or aloud:

Each sip pulls back the curtain some and what I see is yet to come.
Each ripple in the glass defines what's in my heart and yearns to shine.
Each violet drop does shimmer new, its light reflecting all that's true.

May Wine

This traditional Beltane drink—hope and happiness in a glass—originating in Germany with their Maypole celebrations, is infused with the delicate scent of sweet woodruff, resembling a cross between vanilla and honey or sweet hay. Although dried herbs are called for, you can use fresh: double the amount and dry the leaves and flowers (no stems) in the oven on its lowest setting for about 30 minutes, or until it begins to smell fragrant. Drying the herbs brings out their sweet fragrance. May Wine is meant to be drunk while dancing in flower-filled fields, so raise a glass in celebration of youth and young love.

Serves 8

CAUTION: Some people are sensitive to sweet woodruff and it can cause headaches, nausea, and even illness in large amounts. Proceed sensibly and with caution.

½ cup (10 g) dried organic sweet woodruff leaves and flowers

1 bottle (750 ml) light white wine, such as Riesling

1 cup (145 g) fresh strawberries, hulled

1 bottle (750 ml) Champagne or sparkling white wine, chilled

Honey, for sweetening (optional)

While hulling the strawberries, absorb the energies of the seeds that bear success in abundance and imagine where you'll manifest your success. If lucky enough to find a double berry, share it with the one you'd like to fall in love with you.

1. Place the sweet woodruff in a 1-quart (1 L) Mason jar with a lid. Pour in the white wine (save the bottle and cork), seal the jar, and refrigerate overnight.

2. Strain the wine through a fine-mesh sieve back into its original bottle (either using a funnel or glass measuring cup with a spout). Discard the solids.

3. Place a strawberry into each wineglass, filling the glass with intentions of love, fertility, and delight. Fill each glass with 3 ounces (90 ml) of the infused wine, then top off with 3 ounces (90 ml) of Champagne.

4. If you like things a little sweeter, add a drop of honey to taste.

FOR AN ALCOHOL-FREE VERSION: Use a nonalcoholic white wine for the infusion and substitute sparkling water for the Champagne. Note that nonalcoholic wines often still contain a small bit of alcohol. If avoiding alcohol completely, use a sparkling grape juice and top off with sparkling water as needed.

When ready to signal your openness to love and happiness, say quietly or aloud, while sipping the wine:

Each sip of wine breeds love divine;
when said three times, the heart will shine.

Green Man Guac

The ancient Green Man sprouts his leaves each spring as a symbol of rebirth, clearing the way for new growth and the realization of new opportunities. His presence also reminds us to honor Earth in all we do. In recognition of his great wisdom, dish up this Green Man guacamole during your next spring celebration. The avocado supports fertility and possibility; the jalapeño adds a bit of the fire element.

Makes 1 cup (240 g)

---

2 ripe Hass avocados, halved and pitted

1 jalapeño pepper, stemmed and minced

1 Roma tomato, halved, seeded, and finely diced

Juice of 1 lime, plus more as needed

1 teaspoon honey

¼ teaspoon ground coriander

¼ teaspoon kosher salt, plus more as needed

Tortilla chips, pita, jicama slices, cucumber slices, and/or red bell pepper strips, for dipping

Feel the energy contained in the avocado pits—enough to birth a tree! Let it seep into your arms, hands, legs, and feet. Visualize roots and branches growing from you, and imagine how you can use the energy to birth something new in your life.

1. With a grateful heart for the wonder that is Nature, scoop the avocado flesh into a medium bowl and mash with a potato masher or fork until smooth, but still a bit chunky. Stir in the jalapeño, tomato, lime juice, honey, coriander, and salt. Taste and add more lime juice or salt, as needed. Serve with your preferred accompaniments.

2. This is best eaten the day it's made, but you can refrigerate it in an airtight container, sprinkling a bit more lime juice on top to help prevent browning, for up to 1 day.

When ready to honor the possibilities of each new day, and each new leaf it sprouts, say quietly or aloud just before serving:

When leaves do sprout and life turns green,
the sight of watching Nature preen,
instills within a peacock's pride and stirs a joy I just can't hide.
For blessed is each day that brings the chance to plant new seeds again.

Love and Abundance Strawberry Spinach Salad with Poppy Seed Dressing

The green and red colors, strawberry seeds, and poppy seeds in this salad signal love and abundance ahead. Poppy seeds, particularly, stir the imagination, setting the mind to dreaming, and can ease the pain of grief. This delightful salad carries all the energies of spring's optimism and will enrich your kitchen magic as well as your health. The slightly sweet dressing will have you counting your blessings.

Serves 2 as a main course or 4 as a side

FOR THE DRESSING

¼ cup (60 ml) apple cider vinegar or unseasoned rice wine vinegar

2 tablespoons plus 2 teaspoons sugar, divided

½ teaspoon dried minced onion

½ teaspoon ground mustard

¼ teaspoon kosher salt

½ cup (120 ml) olive oil

2 teaspoons poppy seeds

FOR THE SALAD

2 cups (40 g) fresh baby spinach

2 cups (110 g) chopped romaine lettuce

1 cup (170 g) sliced fresh strawberries

½ cup (45 g) thinly sliced red bell pepper

2 tablespoons sliced almonds

*As you prepare the ingredients for this salad to draw abundance to you,
place an almond slice in your pocket for an extra boost of good luck.*

1. To make the dressing: In a blender, combine the vinegar, sugar, onion, mustard, and salt. While processing, slowly pour in the oil and blend until emulsified. Add the poppy seeds and pulse to combine.

2. To assemble the salad: In a large bowl, combine the spinach, romaine, strawberries, and bell pepper. Pour on a generous ¼ cup (60 ml) of dressing and toss to coat and combine. Sprinkle on the almonds—they're the magnet that will attract what you desire. Serve the salad with the remaining dressing on the side.

While preparing, and serving, this salad, say quietly or aloud:

*With each slice and chop I clear the way for magic's glow to fill the day.
Each stir and pour, and sprinkle, too, pulls luck and love and wealth galore.
Each bite, when made with loving care, ensures rewards beyond compare.*

CELEBRATION OF SPRING SOUP

This simple soup can be made with either spring's lovely asparagus or peas and is a celebration in itself of the ease that spring brings, along with the fresh, delicate vegetables now gracing our tables. Its bright green color and eagerly anticipated spring vegetable energy will add a breath of fresh air to any meal it starts. Serve with your favorite crusty bread as an offering to Ostara.

Serves 6

---

3 tablespoons olive oil or unsalted butter

1 large sweet yellow onion, diced

8 cups (1.9 L) chicken or vegetable broth, plus more as needed

Salt and freshly ground black pepper

3 pounds (1.4 kg) fresh asparagus, woody ends trimmed, tips removed and reserved, and stalks roughly chopped, or fresh or frozen peas, thawed

Grated zest of 1 lemon

Fresh herbs for seasoning (basil or thyme with asparagus, or thyme or mint with peas, all for double money luck)

Grated Parmesan cheese, for garnish (optional)

Whether asparagus for its sunny optimism and the patience to await fulfillment of your goals, or peas for family, protection, and abundance, add each to the pot knowing your intentions are heard and trust that the Universe is working on your behalf.

1. Place a soup pot over medium-low heat and pour in the oil (or butter) to warm. Add the onion and cook for 8 to 10 minutes to soften without browning.

2. Pour in the broth, increase the heat, and bring to a boil, then lower the heat to maintain a simmer. Taste the broth and season with salt and pepper.

3. Add the asparagus stalks (or the peas) to the pot and let the liquid return to a simmer. Turn the heat to low, cover the pot, and simmer the soup for 20 to 30 minutes, stirring occasionally, until the vegetables are tender.

4. Carefully transfer the soup in small batches to a standard blender, filling it no more than half full, and blend until smooth. Alternatively, use an immersion blender right in the pot. Return the soup to the pot.

5. Add the reserved asparagus tips, lemon zest, and herbs, stirring clockwise three times. Taste and season again with salt and pepper, as needed. Let simmer for 1 to 2 minutes, until the tips are crisp-tender.

6. Serve with a sprinkle or two of Parmesan, as you like, for increased powers of intuition.

As you ladle the soup into each bowl, say quietly or aloud:

I fill this bowl to nourish that your life be filled with abundance, your soul be filled with joy, your house be full of laughter, and that what's old may seem new and what's new never cease to spark wonder.

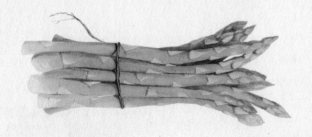

Chocolate-Covered Pineapple

These delicious pineapple treats, when shared, strengthen the bonds of love and friendship, and combined with chocolate that speaks directly to the heart, ensure happy results.

Makes 6 rings or 12 half-rings (half-moons)

NOTE: If your chocolate seizes when melting, use this kitchen witch hack: Slowly stir in some very hot water, about 1 teaspoon at a time, until you have the consistency you need to dip the pineapple.

1 peeled, cored, and sliced fresh pineapple (from your grocery store's produce section) or trimmed, peeled, cored, and chunked fresh pineapple

1 bag (12 ounces, or 340 g) semisweet chocolate chips

1 tablespoon vegetable oil

Kosher salt, for decorating

Unicorn sprinkles, for decorating

Before beginning, clean and tidy your workspace, sharpen your knife, and sample the chocolate to create just the right atmosphere to work your magic.

1. Line a baking sheet with parchment paper and set aside.

2. Cut the pineapple into six 1-inch-thick (2.5 cm) rings, then halve the rings to form half-moons, if desired, or cut the pineapple rings into chunks. Enjoy any leftover pineapple to snack on.

3. Line a cutting board with a clean kitchen towel. Lay the pineapple pieces on the towel and cover with a second towel. Let sit for 30 minutes, gently pressing and blotting the top of the pineapple occasionally. You want to get the slices as dry as possible without pressing out the water. Transfer the pineapple to a plate.

4. Gently melt the chocolate and oil in a double boiler until smooth and liquid.

5. One slice at a time, dip the pineapple in the melted chocolate, covering as much of the slice as you like, then place on the prepared baking sheet. Sprinkle immediately with a pinch of salt or sprinkles (the chocolate will begin to harden quickly). Repeat with the remaining pineapple slices and chocolate.

6. Refrigerate for about 15 minutes, or until hardened. Refrigerate leftovers in an airtight container for up to 2 days.

While dipping each piece of pineapple, say quietly or aloud:

Feel welcome all, here you're covered with love.
Friendship's pure, sweet joy is a gift from above.

SUMMER

This point on the Wheel is full of celebration for the power of light that has triumphed over darkness, but with the knowing truth that darkness will return, and so the need to bask in the Sun's warmth while we can. Celebrating the fleeting joys of summer is a recognition of simple pleasures and living mindfully so as not to miss anything.

The kitchen witch revels in a world filled with choice as Earth offers up her delights. Freshness abounds and breeds excitement and experimentation. For many, life moves outdoors, where we can stretch our limbs and our spirits. Energies are high. A riot of color, flavor, and scent greets us and the manifestation of intentions is everywhere.

Blessings are abundant. Life is good.

A SUMMER
Blessing

As giver of life and all that's new, bright Sun, this blessing honors you.

May warming rays and brilliant light ensure our lives are full and ripe.

The blooms you coax into your gaze bear fruit that yields abundant days.

Each day you rise provides the chance to praise you with our grateful thanks.

ᴸITHA (ᴍIDSUMMER)

This spot on the Wheel of the Year, directly opposite Yule, is fully in the Sun's life-giving focus. Celebrating the longest day of the year, Litha generally occurs about June 21 in the Northern Hemisphere (around December 21 in the Southern), corresponding to the summer solstice when the Sun is at its most powerful, nourishing and nurturing Earth's crops to their full potential. The shadows of Midsummer's Eve, however, foretell that the fairies, newly awakened at Beltane, are now fully active and most mischievous. Protective measures are in order.

Some recognize Litha as a celebration of the Sun King; others, as the time when the Oak King, who represents light, is defeated by his older brother, the Holly King, representing darkness, where he'll rule until winter solstice when the Oak King takes up his reign again. The Catholic Church adopted Litha as the feast day honoring St. John the Baptist. It is also the first official day of summer, which brings a psychological freedom and ease and a sunny optimism—a time when all things are possible.

The element of fire is an important component of midsummer rituals, whether a bonfire, campfire, electric lantern, or other. Following tradition, toss some lavender onto the fire to drive away evil spirits. Growth, expansion, cleansing, and protection, as well as gratitude, are themes of this time on the Wheel of the Year.

For the kitchen witch, it's time to move the kitchen outdoors to enjoy the weather and harness the element of an open flame to cook. If that's not possible, simply move the meal outside, or even open a window wide near your dining table. A hog roast over a bonfire was the traditional culmination of this day of celebration. Other Litha foods include honey, just-picked fresh fruits and vegetables, fresh herbs, and anything spicy and hot. Wherever you eat, the garden is bursting with freshness and your choices are many. Let the gratitude flow for the riches bestowed.

CELEBRATING LITHA

This celebration is all about the Sun, growth, and ease. Channel it in any way that brings you light, joy, warmth, and peace. Some suggestions to get you started:

- Smile, and light someone's day.

- Get outside.

- Make a batch of Sun tea, with herbs from your kitchen garden for extra charm.

- Hang a suncatcher in a window.

- Attract fairies to your garden by incorporating shiny objects, wind chimes, or fresh water.

- Admire the sunset and make a wish—it's sure to come true.

- Evaluate and shine a bit more light on those intentions that are not growing so well.

- Gather fresh herbs to keep the plants producing and honor their efforts by placing them in a vase on your altar, drying them for later use, or incorporating them into your everyday meals.

- Garnish your food and drink with edible flowers in honor of the fairies.

- Walk barefoot . . . in the Sun-warmed grass, on the beach, in your garden . . . and let the protective, grounding energies fill you.

- Watch the busy bees pollinating the trees and plants, then stir a bit of honey into your tea.

- Host a barbecue.

- Have a picnic.

Popping Intentions

Popcorn, one of the oldest forms of corn, is definitely filled with magic, transforming from small, hard kernel to fluffy treat with a little heat and its inherent water: Bam! Inside out in an instant with a burst of energy released into the ether. Why not use that energy to release your intentions to the Universe?

When that popcorn craving calls, make it your preferred way, and don't waste the magical opportunity. While the corn pops, recite your intentions aloud for all to hear and feel them release from your heart into action. Garnish with anything you like to boost the energy.

LAMMAS

Although the temperatures are still quite warm and the Earth is busily producing, you can detect a slight change in the angle of the Sun at this point on the Wheel marking Lammas, as the fall equinox draws ever closer. A celebration of the early harvest and the first of four harvest Sabbats, Lammas (from the Old English *hlaf*, "loaf," and *maesse*, "mass"), August 1 in the Northern Hemisphere (February 1 in the Southern), celebrates the grain harvest. Grains, including corn, were such a critical source of food that festivals, as well as gods and goddesses, were devoted to this sacred gift.

Lammas (alternatively, Lughnasadh, honoring the Celtic god Lugh, guardian of arts and crafts and worshipped as the Sun god) is a day of gratitude for the abundance we reap, marked by a timely harvest to ensure continued sustenance through lean winter months, and brought to life by the first loaves of bread produced that same day, which were then brought to church for blessing. One of the loaves was traditionally broken into four parts, with a piece placed in each corner of the home, or barn, for protection. Symbols of the season represent the harvest, as Earth is full and heavy.

Dating back to Anglo-Saxon times, community gatherings were typical, to celebrate, feast, bargain, and trade goods. Interestingly, the tradition spills over today in the typical appearance of craft festivals and agricultural fairs at this time of year.

For the kitchen witch, the flavors of Lammas are warm from Earth, ripe, juicy, and abundant; the energies thankful, plentiful, and sustaining. During this time of reaping what's been sown, the traditional symbol of Lammas is the scythe or wheat stalk. Traditional foods include bread, beer, berries, corn, rosemary, grapes, sunflowers, and anything cooked over an open flame.

CELEBRATING LAMMAS

There are many ways to celebrate Lammas, but let gratitude be the inspiration behind whatever you choose. A grateful heart leads to mindful living and a happy life that knows no want.

- Use corn kernels to cast an eco-friendly circle to mark your sacred space when practicing your magic outside, such as while cooking or tending your kitchen garden.

- Place a jar of popcorn on your altar to help manifest intentions, along with other seasonal flowers and symbols, using the colors of gold, orange, red, and yellow.

- Write in your gratitude journal about where your intentions have manifested abundance.

- Bake bread.

- Imbue intentions with securing abundance.

- Harvest from your kitchen garden with an offering to Earth, or tidy a patch of Earth in thanks for her gifts.

- Embrace summer's ease before it's gone.

- Craft a corn dolly.

- Share your abundance with others.

The Magic of Summer's Bounty: Glorious, Overflowing, Possibility

Sweet, juicy, ripe, luxurious. Summer's bounty is a time to indulge in the freshness and flavor that abounds. Picnics, parties, barbecues, impromptu celebrations, and informal meals are all the rage as the plenty that exists leaves no room for worries or lack. Spirits are as high as the Sun in the sky as the kitchen witch magically transforms all that's available into a symbol of love, life, friends, and family. The gratitude paid in return is the sweetest blessing.

APRICOT

A member of the rose family, making it appropriate for all
love spells, the delicate apricot was cultivated as far back as
2000 BCE in Central Asia and China, where it was believed
to bestow the gifts of prophecy. Called "seed of the Sun" by the Persians,
apricots spread via travelers along the Great Silk Road and made fans of
everyone they met. Mentioned in *A Midsummer's Night Dream*, apricots
were a sought-after aphrodisiac in Shakespeare's time. This seductress
tempts with juicy sweetness and rewards with a kiss of good luck, success,
and a sunny disposition. Because of its delicate nature, perfectly ripe fruits
are hard to find. Don't pass them by when you do.

BELL PEPPER

The trusty bell pepper, no matter the color, often plays
a supporting role in the kitchen for building flavor and
character in a dish, such as part of the holy trinity in Cajun
cuisine. Let sweet bell pepper support any intentions you imbue into
your cooking for delicious results. Their overall energy is of positivity
and health. Additionally, use **green** for abundance, good luck, growth,
healing, renewal, success; **red** for courage, passion, power, protection,
romantic love, and vitality; **yellow** for communication, confidence,
creativity, happiness, intuition, optimism, personal power, self-esteem,
success in business, and warmth; **orange** for ambition, attraction,
building energy, changing luck, courage, creativity, emotional healing,
health, individuality, joy, and warmth; **purple** for authority, ease,
intuition, wealth, and wisdom; and **hot chile peppers** for change,
initiative, and protection from negative energy.

BLACKBERRY

The blackberry is a part of the rose family, so never
pick them without first asking permission of the
plant's spirit, or those thorns will get you every

Summer's Spice Pantry

Whether seasoning foods with a boost of flavor or intentions, a well-stocked spice pantry is a kitchen witch's ally in magic. Much like spring's pantry, summer's pantry may see spices taking a back seat in your kitchen magic in favor of letting fresh herbs exploding in the garden shine. When the spice pantry is used in summer, the flavors are bright and light with energies of the Sun. Add your favorites to expand the possibilities.

Coriander: to promote healing, health, love, and desire

Cumin: to support emotional strength and new beginnings

Dried chile peppers: to drive change and initiative, instill faithful love, and protect from negative energy

Paprika, sweet or smoked: to boost any spell

Poppy seed: for dream work, intuition, and prosperity

Saffron: to conjure all-purpose magic for what your heart most desires, especially wealth

time. And those thorns are doubly protective against vampires, who supposedly become sidetracked with counting the berries on the bush and forget their evil agenda. Passing under a blackberry bramble arch was said to cure all manner of illness. Blackberry vines, predictably, can be woven into wreaths that grant protection; including rowan and ivy in the wreath seals the deal. The berries represent abundance and prosperity and can be used in all types of culinary applications and traditionally are baked into pies to celebrate Lammas (a.k.a. Lughnasadh). But know it's traditional to leave the first and last harvests on the bushes for the fairies.

BLUEBERRY

Blueberries are native to North America, and the blossom end of the fruit forms a perfect pentagram, imbuing it with magic from the start. Some Indigenous Peoples of northeastern North America believed the Great Spirit sent the "star fruit" to ease hunger, especially for children, during famine.

Blueberries' gorgeous blue color corresponds to the throat chakra and can ease your spirit as well as all manner of communication, instilling it with empathy and honesty. The leaves and the berries are both highly protective and can ward off negative energy attacks. Use blueberries in Moon magic and healing spells. Blueberry tea calms the mind and opens its psychic pathways. Let that blueberry muffin bring peace to your day.

CANTALOUPE

Cantaloupe, called rockmelon in Australia, can be traced back to ancient Greek and Roman times. Because of their fast growth rate, these melons are symbols of fertility and abundance. Cantaloupe's high water content, almost 90 percent, is soothing to the body and spirit, invoking a "go with the flow" attitude that lends ease to our days when they're not going smoothly; its overall energy is of comfort, joy, and sweetness.

CHERRY

Cherries have a lovely reputation for being able to
draw love, and are best used for that purpose in any
kitchen magic recipes. Sipping a tea made from cherry
can open the intuitive pathways and expand your powers of divination.
In Japan, the blossoming cherry tree is a reminder of the impermanence
of life and a universal nudge to stop and appreciate the moment or pay
honor to memories of times or loves now lost from our lives. To ensure
your love is an ingredient in any recipe, use cherrywood spoons to stir
and serve. However cherry is used, it creates a peaceful, loving energy.

CORN

The word *corn* originally was used for any grain.
Corn, also called maize, as in corn on the cob or
the sweet corn we know today, was first grown in
Mexico more than five thousand years ago
and became so important as a food crop to the
Indigenous Peoples of the Americas that there
were gods and goddesses devoted to and worshipped for this sacred gift,
such as Corn Mother (page 32), who is credited with giving her people
sustenance as well as giving them life. Some legends even tell of
people being fashioned from corn. As a sacred food and cultural symbol,
corn was part of many rituals and offerings.

Corn, much like people, does not grow wild; it must be planted,
tended carefully, and cultivated to produce a harvest, and so life
revolved around its planting, nurturing, and harvesting. August's Full
Moon is variously called the Green Corn Moon.

So, too, was corn's importance worldwide, spreading via the Spanish
explorers, that myths and traditions abound:

- In Kentucky, blue grains found among those of a red ear signify
  great good luck.

- British customs hold that the spirit of the corn lives in the last sheaf harvested, which is then turned into a corn dolly that is kept until the next planting season, when it is returned to Earth to ensure a fruitful crop.

- If corn husks are thicker and tougher than usual, prepare for a harsh winter.

- Hanging ears of corn in your kitchen, or bedroom, conjures good, sweet luck.

- The Aztecs believed popping corn released angry spirits.

Corn is a traditional component of the Three Sisters crop—corn, beans, and squash—always planted together, in an early form of companion planting, a technique first used by the Indigenous Peoples of North America, particularly in the northeast. The three plants created synergies, where each plant supported the other in its growth, much as in the happy families this trio suggests.

Though called a vegetable, corn is actually seeds of a type of grass, and symbolizes life, fertility, and spirituality. Its energies are of growth, abundance, grounding, luck, and transformation. It grows in colors of yellow, blue, black, red, and white—even multicolored—and carries the correspondences of each shade. Used in love charms, it calls your beloved to you.

For the kitchen witch, corn offers tremendous versatility in how it can be used. It can be eaten raw or cooked, ground into meal, flour, or starch, made into oil—even popped (definitely magical!). A cob on your altar calls the spirit and strength of Corn Mother.

CUCUMBER

People have been enjoying cucumbers, believed to have originated in India, for at least three thousand years. They were originally thought to be poisonous, and the skin was removed to release the poison. In reality, they're loaded with healthy vitamins and minerals, and this immensely hydrating fruit (not vegetable!) is great for all manner of beauty spells and potions. Cucumbers are an easy-to-grow addition to your kitchen garden, but any stress during growth, just as with people, can cause them to be bitter. The inside temperature of a cucumber can be up to 20 degrees Fahrenheit (-7 degrees Celsius) cooler than the ambient air temperature. So, when you feel your internal temperature rising, take a break and eat some cucumber slices, or down a refreshing glass of cucumber water (combine unpeeled cucumber slices and fresh water in a pitcher and refrigerate until chilled), to regain your equilibrium.

EGGPLANT

A native of India, where it grew wild, this member of the witchy nightshade family was originally much feared, and called the mad apple due to its (perceived) ability to cause insanity—among other maladies. The deep purple color gives eggplant a regal air and can invite success, wealth, wisdom, and spiritual awareness. The original fruit (yes, it's a fruit, actually a berry) was smaller than those we now know, and incredibly bitter, but, just as with humans, some kindness and attention to raising it and preparing it properly gives us the lovely versatile vegetable we enjoy today.

GREEN BEANS

One of the oldest cultivated vegetables, giant beanstalks are not the only magic thing you can grow with green beans. Bolster some money magic with them to increase your wealth, as well as fame and good luck. The plant, with its vining growth habit, represents a tangle of protection. Richer in iron than spinach, green beans will boost your energy so you can tackle all the tasks on your magical to-do list. When planted under a Full Moon, a lush crop is guaranteed. And, much like good intentions left unmanifested, don't let the beans hang on the plant too long or they become tough and difficult to manage.

HERBS

Fresh herbs are at their height of production, flavor, and magic during the summer months. Use them liberally in your kitchen magic to manifest almost any wish.

Basil: Once a sacred herb that women were not allowed to pick, basil has a warming, slightly spicy flavor that makes it a favorite in the kitchen garden, and it's easy to grow indoors if you do not have space for an outdoor garden. In the language of flowers, basil offers good wishes. Let its sweet fragrance waft through your home, spreading a veil of protection from bad energies, while simultaneously stirring fidelity in love and opening the heart to forgiveness. Basil breathes a touch of luck into money spells.

Dill: Love is in the air when dill is in the house. It softly whispers spicy words of lust. The Romans thought it was good luck and fortifying, and covered the foods fed to gladiators with it. The Egyptians used it to repel witches. The Greeks saw wealth in this prolific plant. Dill is doubly magic, giving us both leaves and seeds to use in the kitchen. It is also a vigorous grower and prolific self-seeder, indicating powers of fertility, and its popular use in pickling speaks to its ability to preserve and protect. Female swallowtail butterflies will lay their eggs on dill, which helps feed the caterpillars. What could be more magical than birthing butterflies? Embrace this truly transformative herb.

Lavender: Lavender's timeless scent evokes a sense of calm and happy memories. Its message is of loyalty. When using lavender in culinary applications, such as brewing tea or garnishing iced tea, or baking into cakes and cookies, use only culinary-grade lavender to manifest relaxation, calm, ease, and happiness. Lavender also increases attraction.

Mint: A cleansing herb, mint clears the mind and is said to bring on prophetic dreams, boost concentration, and increase intuitive focus. It can relieve headaches, ease troubling thoughts, and promote renewal.

Oregano: Oregano is said to have been planted by Aphrodite so she could grow joy in her garden. Its flavor is of cozy family meals. Oregano's magical energies can strengthen courage, bring happiness, foreshadow justice, stir love, boost luck, transform stress into tranquility, and help relieve the grief of losing a loved one.

Parsley: Parsley brings invitations of festivity (the ancient Greeks were known to wear parsley crowns to banquets), and just as parsley can cleanse a palate, it can also cleanse unwanted energies from the air and offer protection against ill fates. Parsley presents a conundrum in the romance category: If in love, do not cut parsley for it will cut your connection, but when used to entice romance (if you dare), it is said to promote lust and fertility! Parsley is also associated with good humor, health, and honor.

Rosemary: It is believed that rosemary grows where the sea can be seen, where the righteous abide, or where a woman rules the house. A favorite in the kitchen garden, rosemary promotes love and remembrance, provides clarity, boosts cleansing, increases alertness, fosters fidelity, and repels thieves.

Sage: This is an herb with a long history of healing use and, as its name suggests, sage will bring you wise counsel. A Provençal proverb boasts that any gardener who grows sage will never have need of a doctor! Sage also speaks of all things domestic and the virtues thereof. When sage blossoms in your garden, it beckons hummingbirds to join. From your kitchen apothecary, choose sage to ease grief from the loss of a loved one, promote health and longevity, and grant wisdom, protection, and wishes.

Tarragon: *Tarragon* is from the French *estragon*, or "little dragon"! In the language of flowers, tarragon communicates affection and loyalty. Its anise-like flavor is highly prized in French cuisine and it is part of the classic *fines herbes* seasoning. True to its dragon nature, tarragon inspires courage and confidence and creates feelings of warmth. It can help attract love, keep secrets, and afford protection.

Thyme: Thyme's presence indicates courage, activity, health, and healing. This common garden plant is a workhorse in any witch's kitchen and a favorite of fairies—and rabbits, which are said to smell especially delicious when cooking if they've been eating it. Thyme attracts affection and loyalty. It brings out beauty and courage, protects health, removes negative energy, and promotes sound sleep.

Preserving Summer's Herbal Bounty

Blend your finely chopped fresh herbs of choice with a bit of olive oil to form a paste. Freeze the paste in ice-cube trays. Once solid, transfer to an airtight freezer bag and keep frozen for up to 6 months. Toss into sauces, soups, and stews with a simple nod to their magic.

LIMA BEAN

The story of the lima bean, also sometimes called butter bean, begins in Peru (and, yes, is named for its capital, despite the different pronunciation), and it may be one of the

oldest beans known to the Americas. The lowly lima bean, though, is actually a superfood, loaded with fiber, iron, and protein and an array of micronutrients to boot. These beans are not only good for the body, but they also enrich the soil and surrounding plants with nitrogen they extract from the soil. Part of the Three Sisters of Indigenous North American culture—corn, beans, and squash—they were always grown together for their synergies, proving that a supportive family can get you through rough times with ease. The plant is also able to protect itself from predators and can send signals to other plants nearby that harm is approaching. In that vein, throw a few spare beans on the ground to protect you from negative energies or lurking ghosts. *Phaseolus lunatus*, the scientific name for lima bean, speaks of its lunar shape, telling us of its expansive possibilities. Lima beans can appease our emotions by reducing stress. They are also useful for money magic and can boost creativity (which can certainly help with prosperity!).

MANGO

The sweet, juicy mango is a magical eating experience, enough so to have become the subject of myth, legend, and poetry. Its red and green coloring bursts with passion and abundance. In Indian culture, the mango is revered, and has been for many thousands of years, and was a gift fit for royalty and diplomacy. There, it is known as the King of Fruits and represents happiness and prosperity. It is a symbol of love in Vedic myths. Buddha, it's said, meditated beneath a mango tree in a shady grove given to him purely for that purpose. A mango leaf, placed in a home's entrance, will absorb any negative energy before it enters the home. Whatever your intentions, enchant the mango with them and await your sweet, juicy rewards. When unsure, meditate on it while eating this most delicious fruit.

PEACH

The peach is a cultural icon far beyond Georgia—the Peach State—in the United States. Culturally significant in China (where its origins go as far back as 6000 BCE), Japan, Korea, and Vietnam, peaches are revered for their ability to banish and protect against evil spirits, instill vigor, induce happiness, bestow riches, grant immortality, and invite love—and even deliver babies floating on a river cocooned within a giant peach! In the language of flowers, the peach blossom swoons, "I am your captive!" The fruit bears the message that none is your equal, and when given as a gift delivers quite the compliment. Fallen apricot wood can be carved into a magic wand—or kitchen spoon.

PLUM

The blossoming plum tree, one of the earliest to bloom in spring, marks the turning of the Wheel of the Year and is a sign of beauty, hope, prosperity, and perseverance; its lovely summer fruit, in Japanese lore, is the culmination of the blossom's potential and so, rightly, protects against evil. Its dark purple color speaks of spiritual wisdom and patience.

RASPBERRY

Raspberry's brilliant red color speaks of love and passion in all its forms. Its time to fruit, which only happens after the canes are established for a year, teaches us that patience and careful preparation yield sweet rewards, which, in this case, are carefully protected by thorns (like its cousin the rose), allowing only those who work hard, or approach with respect, to reap. With each plant producing hundreds of berries, sharing the fruits of its labor, the gentle raspberry reminds us that kindness costs nothing and means everything.

SWISS CHARD

Swiss chard is an old soul, perhaps even having grown in the Hanging Gardens of Babylon. This vegetable is relatively easy to grow, not being too temperamental, and can even survive a frost. It's colorful—a veritable rainbow that can activate all the chakras—and some gardens even feature it just for its lovely countenance. It adds flavor to any pot you introduce it to. What more could you ask for in a faithful kitchen companion? Though a member of the beet family, chard is grown for its leaves, not its root, and so making it a good vehicle for spells to bring about change, and quickly, too, or where you need the direct energy of the Sun to instill the stamina to achieve your goals.

TOMATILLO

The tomatillo, also known as the Mexican husk tomato, began its journey to our table in Mesoamerica thousands of years ago, where it was a staple food of the Aztec and Maya peoples. Though its name means "little tomato," it is not actually a tomato, though it is a member of the nightshade family, like the tomato. The tomatillo grows in its own protective cloak, sort of an invisibility cape to protect it from garden predators, and carries strong defensive energies, also evident in its slightly tangy taste.

TOMATO

Another fruit that masquerades as a vegetable (though the U.S. Supreme Court ruled, in 1893, that tomatoes are vegetables, arising from a lawsuit regarding the fact that vegetables, but not fruits, were taxed as imports), the tomato is native to Peru and surrounding areas in the Andes. Despite its astounding popularity and widespread use today, the tomato

encountered slow acceptance as a food when first introduced to Europe in about the sixteenth century. Owing to its association with other—decidedly witchy—plants in the nightshade family, it was deemed poisonous, until proven not so, then proclaimed to be an aphrodisiac—and even lucky.

Because of its nightshade relationship, plants *known* to be used by witches to conjure werewolves, its original scientific name, *Lycopersicon*, translates to "wolf peach." The Italians called it the golden apple, *pomi d'oro*, as early tomatoes were yellow; the French called it the love apple, *pomme d'amour*. The British, who also called it the love apple, took longer to warm up to this lovely than most, and in 1597, herbalist John Gerard scorned it as rank and stinking! Even the French did not adopt the tomato until 1783.

Italy did not know the tomato until the early 1500s, when they eagerly began concocting innumerable uses for it. Aware of its reputation as both poisonous and able to make one mad (and, variously, cause your teeth to fall out), they just boiled the heck out of it, for hours on end, to release the poison, then seasoned liberally with vinegar and spices. (Hmmm, marinara, anyone?!)

The wide variety of colors that tomatoes come in lends a rainbow of magical energies to them. In addition, tomatoes are Sun-loving plants and are infused with that happy correspondence. Tomatoes are associated with Venus and Aphrodite, and so are bountiful in love potions, and they adorn the tables at the first harvest festival of the year. Incorporate into any dish, and watch your money grow. Placed on the mantel or windowsill, the tomato will absorb any negative energy trying to invade the home before it can do you harm.

You need to prune the "suckers" from tomato plants so the plant directs all its energy into producing fruit, not foliage. It's a direct reminder that we need to prune that which no longer serves from our lives to make room for what's new and meaningful to grow.

WATERMELON

Though an ancient fruit, the watermelon's ancestry is a bit murky. Through all its permutations, the sweet juicy fruit we know today is universally loved and reminds us that, although it's good to look back, staying in

the moment to appreciate what's in front of us now is equally, if not arguably more, important.

Watermelon is both cleansing to the body and spirit. Its watery properties tie it to Moon magic and intuition. Use in healing spells and to manifest peace.

ZUCCHINI

Zucchini, and other summer squash, are a traditional component of the Three Sisters crops. Cooperation and support are key energies of this magical vegetable. Zucchini plants are prolific producers, giving us both edible fruit and flowers, and are prime ingredients when abundance is the issue. Its green color is incredibly grounding, yet its watery nature stirs the imagination. Summer squash's edible, thin skins leave them more vulnerable to injury than their thick-skinned winter relatives and remind us that self-care and protection are as important as caring for others.

SEASONAL RECIPES and SPELLS for MAGICAL LIVING

Fresh, easy, informal, and spontaneous are the vibes in the magical kitchen this season. Though the bounty of Earth's gifts would seem to invite a multitude of intentions to manifest (and the opportunity is there to support most any need), remember that your magic works best when focused on those priorities that spring from your heart and will truly make you happy.

Chillingly Good Vibes

Edible flower-studded ice cubes can raise the magic when added to your favorite cheer-boosting beverage. These charming cubes infuse any cold beverage with floral wisdom and good cheer. For fun, and some additional flavor and intention, pair flowers with herbs and pieces of fruit, such as citrus, berries, pineapple, or cranberries. The language of flowers can speak of whatever your heart desires and a toast to those intentions sends your message out to the Universe to be heard and manifested. Cheers!

Makes a varied amount

Edible flowers and blossoms, herb blossoms and sprigs, and leaves to honor your intentions

Wishes whispered to the flower fairies who've donated their flower petals to this endeavor are likely to be granted. Leave a gift of clean water in gratitude.

1. Make sure the foliage you're using is free from dirt and debris. Give it a quick rinse, if needed, and dry well. Arrange edible flower heads and petals, and whatever complementary pieces you've gathered, decoratively in ice-cube-tray compartments.

2. Gently fill the trays about one-third to one-half full of water (use Moon water for more magic!). Use a chopstick or wooden spoon handle to reposition the flowers, as desired, if the water disturbed your arrangement. Carefully transfer the trays to the freezer and freeze for about 1 hour.

3. Fill the trays the remaining way with water and freeze until solid.

As you drop each ice cube into your glass, say quietly or aloud:

Each "clink" does clear the air of harm;
each "clang" a call to do no harm.
Each jangle of the cubes does send "three cheers"
back to what I intend.

CHARMED CHIMICHURRI

Chimichurri's main ingredient, parsley, has a bad reputation as an evil herb—one only grown successfully, especially from seed, by witches. However, it's easy for *anyone* to grow in a sunny spot and is revered for its fresh, bright flavor and healthy dose of vitamin C. This herbal sauce has origins in Argentina, but when made from fresh herbs you've grown (or foraged in the grocery store) and imbued with your intentions, its origins are truly magical. Delightful atop beef, chicken, pork, bruschetta, eggs, or even as a dip for vegetables, this lively condiment spreads your intentions far and wide.

Makes about ¾ cup (170 g)

---

1 cup (60 g) packed fresh parsley leaves

1 tablespoon packed fresh thyme leaves

1 tablespoon packed fresh oregano leaves

1 or 2 cloves garlic, smashed

1 jalapeño pepper, stemmed and coarsely chopped

2 tablespoons olive oil, plus more as needed

2 tablespoons red wine vinegar

1 tablespoon fresh lemon juice

Salt and freshly ground black pepper

Honey, for drizzling (optional)

Working always with gratitude and intention
for whatever your heart desires . . .

1. In a food processor, combine the herbs, garlic, and jalapeño. Pour in the oil, vinegar, and lemon juice and add a pinch of salt and a few grinds of pepper. Pulse to chop, then process until a thick paste-like sauce forms.

2. Transfer the chimichurri to a small bowl. Stirring clockwise with intention, add a drizzle of honey, as an offering to your favorite goddess, if you wish, and a bit more oil to thin the chimichurri to your desired consistency. Refrigerate leftovers in an airtight container for up to 2 days.

Before taking that first bite, inhale the
uplifting aromas and say quietly or aloud:

To keep my magic fresh and bright, I live each day with pure delight.
Each and every simple thing can lift my soul and make it sing.
Each song bears hopes and dreams, I pray,
that manifest in Nature's way.
For as above, then so below, this grateful heart reaps what it sows.

Blackberry Bourbon Besom Cocktail

Blackberries are a tradition at harvest celebrations, and this concoction will definitely help clear the cobwebs and tidy up the attitude. This perfect sipper will ease you into celebration mode and can be an effective way to enhance spellwork: the blackberries will help draw money to you; bourbon, being mostly corn, symbolizes life, fertility, and spirituality; and basil enhances both luck and love. Drink (responsibly) with intention and celebrate the bounty that is yours.

Makes 1 transportive drink

---

5 or 6 large fresh blackberries, or frozen and thawed

2 ounces (60 ml) bourbon

2 large fresh basil leaves

Ice

1 ounce (30 ml) Cointreau

1 ounce (30 ml) sour mix (preferably homemade)

Lemon peel, for garnish

Muddle the ingredients while visualizing crushing any obstacles preventing you from reaching your goals.

In a cocktail shaker, muddle the lucky blackberries, bourbon, and basil to release the juice and essential oils. Fill the shaker with ice and pour in the Cointreau and sour mix. Cover and shake for about 30 seconds to chill. Double strain into a rocks glass over ice. Twist the lemon peel over the glass and add it to the drink. Take a sip and count your blessings.

Before you sip, say quietly or aloud:

O' sweet elixir, bring me luck that manifests in threes:
sip once, and twice, and then again that what I seek does come to me.

H———————H

Succotash Salad

This simple salad celebrates the height of summer's bounty. The name derives from the Narragansett word *msickquatash*, meaning "corn." The Indigenous Peoples of North America introduced this food to the colonists as a gesture of friendship and offer of sustenance. It is a magical dish filled with love, friendship, protection, and abundance.

Serves 4

1 cup (175 g) fresh shelled or frozen lima beans

3 ears sweet corn, shucked, or 2 cups (270 g) frozen kernels, thawed

2 tablespoons olive oil, plus more as needed

Honey, for seasoning

1 red bell pepper, cored, seeded, and diced

2 Roma tomatoes, seeded and chopped

¼ cup (10 g) fresh basil leaves, cut into chiffonade

Juice of 1 lime, plus more to taste

Freshly ground black pepper

As you prepare the vegetables and herbs, savor the fresh aromas and vibrant colors and let them lift your spirits. Take stock of where some "freshness" may be a good addition to your life.

1. Cook the lima beans according to the package directions. Drain and set aside.

2. While the beans cook, carefully cut the kernels from the corncobs.

3. In a large skillet over medium-high heat, warm the oil. Add the corn and a drizzle or two of honey to boost the prosperity of the dish and honor the community of bees that created it, and cook, stirring frequently, for 6 to 8 minutes, until the corn begins to soften and take on some brown color from the sugars caramelizing.

4. Turn the heat to medium, add the bell pepper, and cook, stirring occasionally, for about 3 minutes, or until the pepper softens a bit. Stir in the lima beans, clockwise, and remove from the heat.

5. Gently stir in the tomatoes, basil, juice of 1 lime, and pepper to taste. Taste and add more lime juice or a drizzle of oil, as needed. Serve warm or at room temperature.

While preparing this food, when ready, say quietly or aloud:

Earth, Sun, wind, and rain produce this bounty that sustains.
Abundance speaks and calls us home, that all within do cease to roam.
For bounty grows in many ways when love and friendship lead the way.

Basil Balsamic Vinegar

Add a dash of magic to any meal with a sprinkle of basil balsamic vinegar. Basil's magical properties are good for, among other things, fostering family love and boosting luck, and the vinegar bears grapes' energies of stress relief and the fluidity of the Moon's influence to adapt and change. This magical elixir is for more than just salads—dress grilled meats or vegetables, drizzle over fresh tomatoes and mozzarella or pizza, or dip in a crusty bread or fresh vegetables for a flavor-filled appetizer and a peaceful family meal.

Makes about 2 cups (480 ml)

---

1 cup (40 g) packed fresh basil leaves, gently washed and thoroughly dried (water promotes bacterial growth)

2 cups (480 ml) good-quality balsamic vinegar, plus more as needed

The act of sprinkling this vinegar on your food
is as important as the act of sprinkling water on your altar
as a form of blessing and intention. Food is sacred.

1. Wash and thoroughly dry one 28-ounce (840 ml) Mason jar and one pint-size (475 ml) Mason jar and their lids.

2. Gently bruise or crush the basil to help release the oils. Place the basil in the larger jar, leaving 1 to 2 inches (2.5 to 5 cm) of space at the top. Pour the vinegar over the basil, making sure the basil's covered. Cover the jar with a lid and set aside in a cool, dark place for up to 2 weeks to infuse the vinegar with the basil's sweet touch. After 3 or 4 days, taste the vinegar to judge how intense the herbal flavor is. You may want to taste it each day until it develops the flavor you like.

3. Place a fine-mesh sieve over the pint-size (475 ml) jar and strain the vinegar into it. Discard the basil. Seal the lid tightly. Store in a cool, dark place for up to 1 year. If the vinegar shows any signs of change or deterioration, such as mold growth, discard immediately and do not use.

While charging any meal, or individual ingredients to satisfy everyone's taste, with this vinegar, say quietly or aloud:

A dash of basil for great courage when rocky roads prevail.
A cleansing splash of vinegar to keep safe along life's trail.
So, taste and stir and add some more, meant just for flavor's sake—
my wish for you, a seasoned life, is there for you to take.

COVEN OF THE MOONBEAM RAVINE'S CHILI SAUCE

An ancient (and secret until now) recipe passed down from the great-grandmother of the coven's founder, this savory sauce is a must to spice up any gathering. Whether used to awaken the flavors of foods or reveal your heart's true desires, this sauce speaks with the loving-kindness of the hands that have made it. It can dress any protein with its magic, like pork, beef, chicken, or eggs, and vegetables delight in its attention. Stir it into sauces for even more dazzle. Its versatility will enchant and its wisdom will be absorbed with every bite. Use wisely, for its magic is powerful.

Makes about 6 pints (about 454 g each); recipe can be halved but may require less time to cook

16 large, ripe tomatoes (8 to 9 pounds, or 3.6 to 4 kg, total)

3 large green bell peppers, cored, seeded, and chopped

2 large sweet onions, chopped

1 or 2 jalapeño peppers, stemmed and diced

2 cups (480 ml) apple cider vinegar

2 cups (400 g) granulated sugar

1 tablespoon kosher salt

2 teaspoons ground allspice

2 teaspoons ground ginger

2 teaspoons freshly grated nutmeg

2 teaspoons ground cloves

2 teaspoons ground mustard

Dash of ground cinnamon

Always stir clockwise to bring what you desire to you and utilize the inactive time to set your intentions and plan your actions to align.

1. Utilizing the transformative power of fire, bring a large pot of water to a boil over high heat. While the water boils, fill a large bowl with water and ice, about half and half. With the tip of a sharp paring knife, carefully cut an X into the bottom of each tomato. Drop the tomatoes, 2 or 3 at a time, into the boiling water. Boil for 30 seconds to 1 minute until the skin starts to peel back at the X. Transfer to the ice bath, let cool, and remove. Repeat with the remaining tomatoes.

2. Slip the skins off the cooled tomatoes, halve them, and gently squeeze out the seeds. Coarsely chop the tomatoes and transfer to a large pot or Dutch oven. Add the bell peppers, onions, and jalapeño. Place the pot over low heat.

3. In a saucepan over medium heat, combine the vinegar, sugar, salt, and spices. Bring to a boil while stirring frequently to dissolve the sugar and spices. Pour the vinegar mixture into the tomato mixture and mix well. Turn the heat to medium-high and bring the chili sauce to a boil, stirring occasionally.

4. Reduce the heat to maintain a simmer, place the lid on the pot slightly ajar, and cook for about 3 hours, stirring occasionally, until reduced and thickened to your liking.

5. Let cool completely before transferring to clean jars with tight-fitting lids or airtight containers. Keep refrigerated for about 2 weeks (discard if any signs of mold appear), or freeze for up to 6 months (leaving at least 1 inch, or 2.5 cm, of headspace in the jars for expansion). Thaw in the refrigerator.

As you stir the mixture, say quietly or aloud:

Into this cauldron do I wield the fruits and seeds of harvest's yield:
Tomatoes will bring love and grace, while
peppers grant a change of pace.
Sweet onions clear the mind and nose and
help you see the path you chose.
The yin and yang of sweet and sour bring balance to the witching hour.
With salt and spices to protect, these potent charms do intersect,
and brewed to grant your sacred wish, a blessed life you can expect.

Soothing Lavender White Chocolate Shortbread

There is nothing "short" on flavor—or magic—here. These buttery, sweet, slightly floral treats are the perfect accompaniment to a quiet cup of tea and a divination ritual. Let the lavender soothe your mind and spirit and awaken your intuition as you prepare to take a peek into the future. White chocolate keeps things light and happy. When given as a gift from your kitchen, lavender signifies friendship and peace.

Makes 16 shortbread wedges

1½ teaspoons dried culinary-grade lavender buds

1 cup (2 sticks, or 225 g) unsalted butter, at room temperature

½ cup (100 g) plus 1 tablespoon granulated sugar, divided

½ cup (50 g) confectioners' sugar

1 teaspoon vanilla extract

2 cups (240 g) all-purpose flour

½ teaspoon kosher salt

1 cup (175 g) white chocolate chips

Breathe in lavender's heady aroma and let it mix with your breath, absorbing and carrying away any negativity or tenseness you feel and centering you fully in this delicious moment.

1. Line a 9-inch (23 cm) tart pan with a removable bottom with a parchment round.

2. Finely crush the lavender between two sheets of wax paper with a rolling pin, or in a mortar and pestle, and transfer to a large bowl.

Add the butter. Using an electric handheld mixer, whip the butter and lavender on medium speed for about 2 minutes, or until well blended and fluffy.

3. Add ½ cup (100 g) of the granulated sugar, the confectioners' sugar, and vanilla and beat on medium speed until well blended and light, stopping to scrape the sides of the bowl as needed.

4. Add the flour and salt and beat, starting on low speed and increasing to medium, until blended. Mix in the chocolate chips until evenly distributed. The dough will be crumbly. Transfer the dough to the prepared pan (it will be full), then use a flat-bottomed glass or measuring cup to press it evenly into the pan. Using a sharp knife, lightly score the shortbread into 16 wedges. Refrigerate for 1 hour.

5. Preheat the oven to 300°F (150°C, or gas mark 2).

6. Bake for 50 to 60 minutes, until firm and just a touch of golden color forms around the edges. Remove from the oven and sprinkle the shortbread with the remaining 1 tablespoon of granulated sugar. Let the shortbread cool completely, remove the rim of the pan, and cut the shortbread along the score lines. Store in an airtight container for up to 1 week.

Though probably not potent enough to bring world peace, these cookies can bring a little peace to your world. Before taking the first soothing bite, take a deep breath in and release it slowly, then say quietly or aloud:

I breathe in peace, I breathe out woe,
and welcome calm, my pulse to slow.
The moment now is rich and full, its sweetness like a soothing lull.
In lavender's rich scent you'll find
your dreams revealed, a life sublime.

ℰPILOGUE

The Wheel has turned its final turn, to end this year where much was learned.

We've sown and grown and reaped galore, but have no fear: much more's in store.

For what was once a pot, a pan, conjures magic in a witch's hand.

I hope you see each fruit, each seed, as something more than just to feed.

Each vegetable, each herb, each tree, invites the chance to really see

that magic lives in everything—just waiting for your summoning.

But the end is not the end, my sweet, for born again, the Wheel repeats.

Each season, then, a chance anew to manifest with all you do;

each celebration ripe for change with echoes of time-honored ways.

Don't hide your magic—let it shine, for life is short and you're divine.

With fire, water, earth, and air, your powers grow beyond compare.

When handled by the kitchen witch, those powers can grant any wish.

ACKNOWLEDGMENTS

Each book has its own recipe for success and I owe great thanks to the talented "kitchen brigade" who helped bring this one to fruition.

To Quarto publisher Rage Kindelsperger, my immense and heartfelt thanks for lighting the fire from which these words do spring and nurturing their growth with faith and expert guidance.

To Elizabeth You, for carefully tending the cauldron to ensure the manuscript was seasoned properly and finished on time. And to Karen Levy, for adding just the right garnishes.

To all the teams at Quarto, for their dedication to supporting authors and their incredible talents to bring beautiful books into the world.

To all my friends and family who cast magic into my life, and kitchen, daily, thank you for your love and support.

To John, for the spice that keeps life fun and the love that keeps it real.

Finally, the world would be such a dull place without the magic of books. It is a magic multiplied exponentially each time a reader opens one and brings their own magic to it.

References & Resources

Atlas Obscura: atlasobscura.com.

Beltane Fire Society: Beltane.org.

Bremness, Lesley. *The Complete Book of Herbs*. New York: Viking Studio/Penguin Putnam, Inc., 1988.

Chadd, Rachel Warren. "The Folklore of Eggs: Their Mystical, Powerful Symbolism." https://folklorethursday.com/myths/folklore-eggs-mystical-powerful-symbolism. Accessed October 26, 2022.

Civitello, Linda. *Cuisine & Culture: A History of Food and People*. 3rd ed. Hoboken, NJ: John Wiley & Sons, Inc., 2011.

Cottingham, Karen. "Gingerbread." The Herb Society of America—South Texas Unit. www.herbsociety-stu.org/gingerbread.html. Accessed October 26, 2022.

Culpeper, Nicholas. *The Complete Herbal*. London: Thomas Kelly, 1850. The Project Gutenberg eBook #49513, July 24, 2015. Gutenberg.org.

Cunningham, Scott. *Cunningham's Encyclopedia of Magical Herbs*. Woodbury, MN: Llewellyn Publications, 1985, 2000.

Cunningham, Scott. *Cunningham's Encyclopedia of Wicca in the Kitchen*. Woodbury, MN: Llewellyn Publications, 2003.

Denker, Joel S. *The Carrot Purple and Other Curious Stories of the Food We Eat*. Lanham, MD: Rowman & Littlefield, 2015.

Dugan, Frank M. *Hidden Histories and Ancient Mysteries of Witches, Plants, and Fungi*. St. Paul, MN: American Phytopathological Society, 2015.

Farmers' Almanac: farmersalmanac.com.

Folkard, Richard. *Plant Lore, Legends, and Lyrics: Embracing the Myths, Traditions, Superstitions, and Folk-Lore of the Plant Kingdom*. The Project Gutenberg eBook #44638, January 9, 2014. Gutenberg.org.

Guiley, Rosemary Ellen. *The Encyclopedia of Magic and Alchemy*. New York: Facts on File, 2006.

Herbst, Sharon Tyler, and Ron Herbst. *The New Food Lover's Companion*. 5th ed. Highland Ranch, CO: Peterson's Publishing LLC, 2013.

Kent, Cicely. *Telling Fortunes by Tea Leaves: How to Read Your Fate in a Teacup*. The Project Gutenberg ebook #6964, March 21, 2013. Gutenberg.org.

Library of Congress: LOC.gov.

Meyer, Danny. *Union Square Cafe Cookbook: 160 Favorite Recipes from New York's Acclaimed Restaurant*. New York: Ecco, 2013.

National Geographic: nationalgeographic.com.

National Trust: nationaltrust.org.uk.

Nurin, Tara. "How Women Brewsters Saved the World." Craft Beer & Brewing. April 21, 2016. https://beerandbrewing.com/how-women-brewsters-saved-the-world. Accessed November 4, 2022.

The Practical Herbalist: https://thepracticalherbalist.com.

Shakespeare, William. *A Midsummer Night's Dream*. 1600.

Skalicky, Francis. "Facts of Persimmons as Interesting Folklore." Missouri Department of Conservation. *Springfield News-Leader*, October 5, 2018. www.news-leader.com/story/sports/outdoors/2018/10/05/facts-persimmons-interesting-folklore/1486574002.

Smithsonian Institution, National Museum of Natural History: https://naturalhistory.si.edu.

Toussaint-Samat, Maguelonne. *A History of Food*. Chichester, U.K: Wiley-Blackwell, 2009.

Tumacácori National Historical Park. "Ethnobotany of Fruit Trees." National Park Service. https://www.nps.gov/articles/000/ethnobotany-of-fruit-trees.htm. Accessed November 4, 2022.

United States Department of Agriculture: USDA.gov.

University of Illinois Extension: https://web.extension.illinois.edu.

Winick, Stephen. "Ostara and the Hare: Not Ancient, but Not as Modern as Some Skeptics Think." Library of Congress, Folklife Today. https://blogs.loc.gov/folklife/2016/04/ostara-and-the-hare. Accessed October 26, 2022.

World History Encyclopedia: worldhistory.org.

INDEX

For John

First published in 2023 by Wellfleet Press,
an imprint of The Quarto Group,
142 West 36th Street, 4th Floor,
New York, NY 10018, USA
T (212) 779-4972 F (212) 779-6058
www.Quarto.com

Wellfleet titles are also available at discount for retail, wholesale, promotional, and bulk purchase. For details, contact the Special Sales Manager by email at specialsales@quarto.com or by mail at The Quarto Group, Attn: Special Sales Manager, 100 Cummings Center Suite 265D, Beverly, MA 01915 USA.

10 9 8 7 6 5 4 3 2 1

ISBN: 978-1-57715-343-6

Library of Congress Control Number: 2023932579

Publisher: Rage Kindelsperger
Creative Director: Laura Drew
Managing Editor: Cara Donaldson
Editor: Elizabeth You
Cover and Interior Design: Laura Klynstra

Printed in China